RenderScript: parallel computing on Android, the easy way

Android is beautiful because you can hack it

Alberto Marchetti

alberto.marchetti@hydex11.net
https://www.linkedin.com/in/albertomarchetti

RenderScript: parallel computing on Android, the easy way

Special thanks

I want to thank:

> **Danial Jafari Giv**[1], who helped me all along the discovery of this framework, and whose theoretical support has been a deep relief for my mind.
> **Luigi Villa**[2], who is one of the most tenacious developers I have ever met. Our continuous discussions brought up a lot of the details that enrich this book.
> **Graham Reynolds**[3], who reviewed and edited this book, exercising his knowledge to make my dream come true.

---

[1] Danial Jafari Giv - LinkedIn - https://www.linkedin.com/in/danial-jafarigiv-323a1442
[2] Luigi Villa - LinkedIn - https://www.linkedin.com/in/luigi-villa-b71a984
[3] Graham Reynolds - LinkedIn - https://www.linkedin.com/in/graham-reynolds-2934169

Table of contents

Introduction

This book explains the basics of RenderScript framework usage. I had the idea of writing this book in December 2015, when I had to build a fast ORB features[4] extractor for Android mobile phones (in the field of augmented reality, this kind of topic is researched a lot, because optimizing computer vision algorithms on mobile is mandatory to achieve good real time results). The RenderScript topic came out to be peculiar, with not so much documentation around, and the goal was challenging. After having looked around for RenderScript documentation, I came up with a simple list of available articles:

Intel's RenderScript Basic Tutorial for Android OS[5]
A basic tutorial that shows how to implement a kernel that works over an image and responds to users' touch. It is useful to understand a few core concepts, like how to write a simple script.

Google's RenderScript introduction[6]
Google's introduction, which shows basic features of RenderScript and how to set it up. This is another good resource to understand the basics of the framework, as well as some more deep concepts (reading, for example, Google's Android Developers Blog[7]).

Android NDK: Beginner's Guide - Second Edition[8]
A really good Android NDK book. It contains a chapter talking about how to implement a RenderScript C++ NDK side script.

Parallelization Strategy Based on RenderScript Reductions[9]
This is a paper that "proposes several strategies for reduction algorithms implementation between vectors using RenderScript". It shows timing benefits of applying RenderScript to calculation problems.

Also, it is possible to analyze RenderScript available documentation directly from Android's website[10] and from its source code's `.spec`[11] files. Analyzing the source code directly has been the most straightforward way for me to understand exactly how this wonderful framework works.

Also, StackOverflow[12] has been a good source of information to get the grasp on common problems.

Once I understood that there was not a place where you can find tons of useful information about RenderScript, the idea of writing this book came up. The first edition of this book tries to cover as much as possible both general and deep topics, to help developers get a grasp immediately on the RenderScript topic.

Who this book is for

This book is written for developers who want to understand how to do parallel computing on Android devices. It is mainly recommended to developers who have at least some general experience of Java/Android development (Google itself provides a simple tutorial[13] and C pointers basic knowledge (TutorialsPoint provides a good tutorial[14]).

---

4 Ethan Rublee, Vincent Rabaud, Kurt Konolige, Gary Bradski - ORB: an efficient alternative to SIFT or SURF - http://www.vision.cs.chubu.ac.jp/CV-R/pdf/Rublee_iccv2011.pdf
5 Intel's RenderScript Basic Tutorial for Android OS - https://software.intel.com/sites/default/files/managed/36/bc/AndroidBasicRenderScript_0.pdf
6 Google's RenderScript introduction - http://developer.android.com/guide/topics/renderscript/index.html
7 Android Developers Blog - http://android-developers.blogspot.it/
8 Android NDK: Beginner's Guide - Second Edition - https://books.google.it/books?id=cWK4CAAAQBAJ
9 Parallelization Strategy Based on RenderScript Reductions - http://rcs.cic.ipn.mx/rcs/2014_78/Parallelization%20Strategy%20Based%20on%20RenderScript%20Reductions.pdf
10 Android's website - http://developer.android.com/guide/topics/renderscript/reference/overview.html
11 RenderScript source code - `.spec` - https://android.googlesource.com/platform/frameworks/rs/+/marshmallow-mr1-release/api/
12 StackOverflow - Search for "RenderScript" - http://stackoverflow.com/search?tab=newest&q=renderscript
13 Google simple Android development tutorial - http://developer.android.com/training/basics/firstapp/index.html
14 TutorialsPoint C pointers tutorial - http://www.tutorialspoint.com/cprogramming/c_pointers.htm

Also, basic understanding of parallel computing paradigms is encouraged (Lawrence Livermore National Laboratory provides an introduction to parallel computing[15]), to understand how to translate a serial program to a parallel one.

If you want to discuss your RenderScript work and problems, there is an opened topic on Quora: RenderScript - Parallel Computing on Android[16]

What is parallel computing?

Parallel computing is a way of performing calculations in a concurrent manner, instead of performing them in a serial process. Its benefit is seen when calculations are done in parallel over a large set of elements: it usually means performing the same kind of operation over every element of the set. Devices that have a large number of cores, like GPUs, are extremely suitable to handle this kind of work; to better understand the concept, let's consider the following example:

> A function, named foo, takes 1ms to be executed on a CPU core and 3ms to be executed over a GPU one.
> foo has to be applied over a set counting 1,048,576 elements.
> There can be only 8 CPU cores running simultaneously and 256 GPU ones.

CPU side

The required number of total CPU parallel cycles is:

```
parallelCycles(cpu) = 1,048,576 / 8 = 131,072
```

Consumed time on the CPU side is:

```
elapsedTime(cpu) = parallelCycles(cpu) * 1ms = 131,072ms ~= 131s
```

GPU side

The required number of total GPU parallel cycles is:

```
parallelCycles(gpu) = 1,048,576 / 256 = 4,096
```

Consumed time on GPU side is:

```
elapsedTime(gpu) = parallelCycles(gpu) * 3ms = 12,288ms ~= 12s
```

Result

It is easy to see that running the function over a GPU device, despite having slower cores than a CPU, can benefit calculations over big sets of elements.

For deeper info, please refer to online articles, like Wikipedia - Parallel computing[17] or NVIDIA - Accelerated Computing[18].

What is needed to use this book

All that is needed to use this book is:

> Android Studio[19], as everything here talks about Android and as it is the official Android IDE, distributed by Google and based upon JetBrain's IntelliJ IDEA[20].
> (Optional) Android NDK[21], if you plan to test native RenderScript access.

---

[15] Lawrence Livermore National Laboratory - Introduction to parallel computing - https://computing.llnl.gov/tutorials/parallel_comp/
[16] Quora: RenderScript - Parallel Computing on Android - https://www.quora.com/topic/RenderScript-Parallel-Computing-on-Android
[17] Wikipedia - Parallel computing - https://en.wikipedia.org/wiki/Parallel_computing
[18] NVIDIA - Accelerated Computing - https://developer.nvidia.com/accelerated-computing-training
[19] Android Studio - http://developer.android.com/sdk/index.html
[20] IntelliJ IDEA - https://www.jetbrains.com/idea/

Author thoughts

Parallel computing on mobile is currently (2016) not yet a not trending topic, because, to make a simple comparison, a high end desktop GPU (Nvidia GeForce GTX 980) provides around 4612 GFLOPS[22] of processing power, while a high end mobile phone (Samsung S6, uses Mali-T760 MP8 GPU) provides around 190 GFLOPS[23]. This means that the desktop GPU totally outperforms mobile ones by at least a 20x factor.

Usage of parallel computing on mobile phones, then, **should relate to mobile-specific operations**.

The following scenario will help you better understand the concept:

Scenario
We analyze mobile-phone camera-captured (provided at runtime) images to detect human faces in the environment. Detected faces are needed for a back-end service.

Without parallel computing
We transfer, from mobile-device to back-end, 1 frame every 5 seconds (to preserve bandwidth), which needs to be of good enough quality, consuming around 2 megabytes of bandwidth in a minute. Then, we process the provided images in back end.

With parallel computing
We pre-analyze the images directly on the phone, and perform face detection, saving a file containing the definition of every face we get. We transfer 1 compressed file every 2 seconds (to preserve battery life, as analysis is computationally expensive), consuming around 90KB of bandwidth. Then, we process faces data in back end.

As you can see, in order to obtain the same result, two different approaches can be used. For the mobile phones market, which has strong bandwidth limits, the parallel computing approach would be more suitable.

How this book is structured

What is RenderScript
Here a general discussion is provided about RenderScript, the right way to set it up and a first example to see it working.

RenderScript components
You can find a detailed explanation involving a good number of RenderScript components, both required and optional ones. Also inside this chapter comes a small summary involving FilterScript, a subset of RenderScript made for optimal GPU performance.

Performance notes
In this section a discussion is presented about RenderScript components' performance.

Native analysis
This brief chapter is a fast reference to explore under-the-hood RS source code.

RenderScript and NDK
This chapter tackles the specific needs to access an RS Allocation and invoking RS kernels from the Android NDK side. Also, a general overview about how to use RenderScript's NDK native implementations is given.

Use cases
Here is a list of working examples (with complete sample project) for different use cases.

Porting case - FAST features detection
In this chapter a porting process is presented, which can make FAST features extraction work inside RenderScript.

---

[21] Android NDK - http://developer.android.com/ndk/index.html
[22] Wikipedia - NVIDIA GeForce 900 series - https://en.wikipedia.org/wiki/GeForce_900_series#Products
[23] kyokojap - GPU GFLOPS - http://kyokojap.myweb.hinet.net/gpu_gflops/#td_5_56

Conclusions
The conclusions of the book.

Appendix - *API changes*
Over different Android versions, RenderScript API has changed: here a list of relevant changes is provided from API 19 onwards.

Appendix - *Enable NDK support*
A brief reference on how to set up Android NDK on the latest Android Studio versions.

Appendix - *Other Android parallel computing frameworks*
A discussion about other available Android-based parallel computing frameworks.

Source code

All our sample projects can be found inside this book's public repository[24].

If you find any problems with the code, please report them into the issues tracker[25].

---

[24] Book's public repository - https://bitbucket.org/cmaster11/rsbookexamples/src
[25] Book's issues tracker - https://bitbucket.org/cmaster11/rsbookexamples/issues

What is RenderScript

There is no one better than Google at explaining what their systems can do:

RenderScript is a framework for running computationally intensive tasks at high performance on Android. RenderScript is primarily oriented for use with data-parallel computation, although serial computationally intensive workloads can benefit as well. **The RenderScript runtime will parallelize work across all processors available on a device, such as multi-core CPUs, GPUs, or DSPs, allowing you to focus on expressing algorithms rather than scheduling work or load balancing.** *RenderScript is especially useful for applications performing image processing, computational photography, or computer vision.*

To read Google's complete RenderScript overview, visit its homepage[26]. For a general reference about RenderScript Java API, please visit Google's RenderScript API Reference[27].

RenderScript is a huge library. It embeds parallel computing (like CUDA) as well as graphical production power (to operate with OpenGL 3D contexts). In this book the main talk will be about its pure parallel computing features.

Note: as Google itself states in RenderScript documentation[28], **The graphics subsystem of RenderScript was removed at API level 23**. There are other, more performing ways, like pure OpenGL ES[29] or Vulkan[30], to handle graphics concepts. RenderScript should be used mainly as a parallel computing language.

Experience-based API Note

In this book the **Min Android API 18** will be used because, with a market share greater than 70% (API >= 18), this API is perfect for real-time purposes: targeting old devices is not suitable as low processing power cannot be easily dealt with by RenderScript. As said later, in the *Support Library section*, there is a library that lets you use RenderScript on old devices. In the book, it will only be used inside the SurfaceRenderExample sample project[31]. RenderScript source code will refer to the latest version available at this time, `marshmallow-mr1-release`[32].

For your info, Android latest versions market share[33] chart (as of March 7, 2016) is the following:

Version	Name	API	Distribution
4.3	Jelly Bean	18	3.2%
4.4	KitKat	19	34.3%
5.0	Lollipop	21	16.9%
5.1	Lollipop	22	19.2%
6.0	Marshmallow	23	2.3%

How RenderScript works

The whole concept is easy. For example, if your software's input is an array of numbers, and you want to increment each one by a certain value, the workflow is as follows:

1. Define a RenderScript **Context**.
2. Create a RenderScript **Script**, containing a **Kernel** function that computes your required increment.

---

[26] Android developers - RenderScript - http://developer.android.com/guide/topics/renderscript/index.html
[27] Google's RenderScript API Reference - http://developer.android.com/reference/android/renderscript/package-summary.html
[28] RenderScript docs - `rs_graphics` - http://developer.android.com/guide/topics/renderscript/reference/rs_graphics.html
[29] OpenGL ES - Wikipedia - https://en.wikipedia.org/wiki/OpenGL_ES
[30] Vulkan - Wikipedia - https://en.wikipedia.org/wiki/Vulkan_(API)
[31] SurfaceRenderExample sample project - https://bitbucket.org/cmaster11/rsbookexamples/src/tip/SurfaceRenderExample/
[32] `marshmallow-mr1-release` - RenderScript source code -
https://android.googlesource.com/platform/frameworks/rs/+/marshmallow-mr1-release/
[33] Android latest versions market share - http://developer.android.com/about/dashboards/index.html

3. Load your input numbers inside an input **Allocation**.
4. Define an output allocation that matches the **Type** of the input one.
5. Execute the kernel function on the input allocation.
6. Copy the contents of the output allocation to an array and there you have your output numbers.

How many new words! Let's take a look at their meanings:

Context
A **Context** has for RenderScript the same meaning that it has for an Android Activity. RenderScript scripts initialized inside the same context will be able to access the same Allocations.

Script
RenderScript code is written into compilable files, which use a **C99**[34] programming language variant (having extensions `.rs`, `.fs`).

Allocation
A RenderScript allocation is a class that interfaces with a memory allocation (the one you create using the C `malloc`[35] function) where you can store your scripts' data. An allocation is defined by a root element (which tells RS what kind of data you are storing inside the allocation) and the count of those elements.

Kernel
A RenderScript kernel is a function applied to every allocation's element and does calculations over it.

Type
A RenderScript Type defines which kind of basic element an allocation has (e.g. `int`) and the dimensions of the allocation itself (like x, y and z).

To get a deeper understanding of these objects, please refer to the *RenderScript components* chapter.

First example

To better understand the whole concept, let's build a full example on how to increment numbers that are inside an array. You can find an example of this process inside our FirstExample sample project[36].

Setup RenderScript

> Create a new Android project.
> Edit its `build.gradle` file:

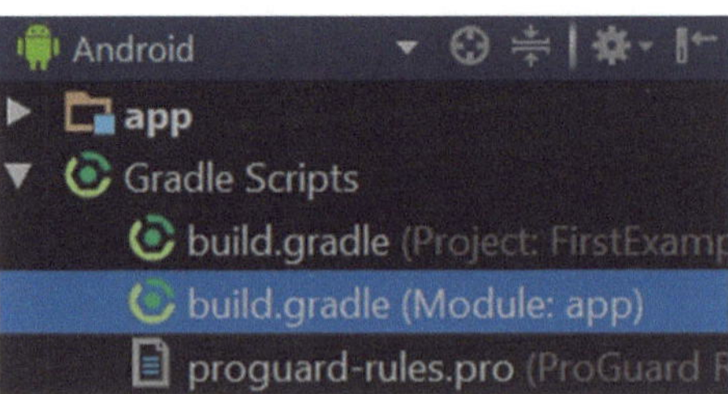

`build.gradle` *file location*

> Change the android section to have values greater or equal to the following:

```
compileSdkVersion 23

// Reference:
// https://code.google.com/p/android/issues/detail?id=71347#c31
```

---

[34] C99 - Wikipedia - https://en.wikipedia.org/wiki/C99
[35] `malloc` - cplusplus.com - http://www.cplusplus.com/reference/cstdlib/malloc/
[36] FirstExample sample project - https://bitbucket.org/cmaster11/rsbookexamples/src/tip/FirstExample/

```
// Build tools 23.0.1 broke RenderScript functioning, so minimum value is as follows:
buildToolsVersion "23.0.2"
```

» Change the `android.defaultConfig` section to have the `minSdkVersion` value greater or equal to 18:

```
minSdkVersion 18
```

» Add, inside the `android.defaultConfig` section, the following line:

```
renderscriptTargetApi 18
```

Note: it's possible to target old devices, having API lower than 18. For this case, you should use the *RenderScript support library*, which brings many newer features back to API 8 powered devices.

Note: `renderscriptTargetApi` key is extremely relevant when compiling your applications, because it enables or disables certain RS functions. To see what changed through time, please refer to the *API changes* appendix. This value should be set equal to the `minSdkVersion`, because if incompatible API is detected, the following error will be thrown (example applies for `renderscriptTargetApi` set to 23, running on an Android 21 device):

```
E/bcinfo: Invalid API version: 23 is out of range ('11' - '21')
E/RenderScript: Failed to translate bitcode from version: 23
...
android.renderscript.RSRuntimeException: Loading of ScriptC script failed.
```

> Right-click on your app module, inside the `1: Project` sidebar, and create a new RenderScript folder, using the `New -> Folder -> RenderScript Folder` menu item (as shown below).

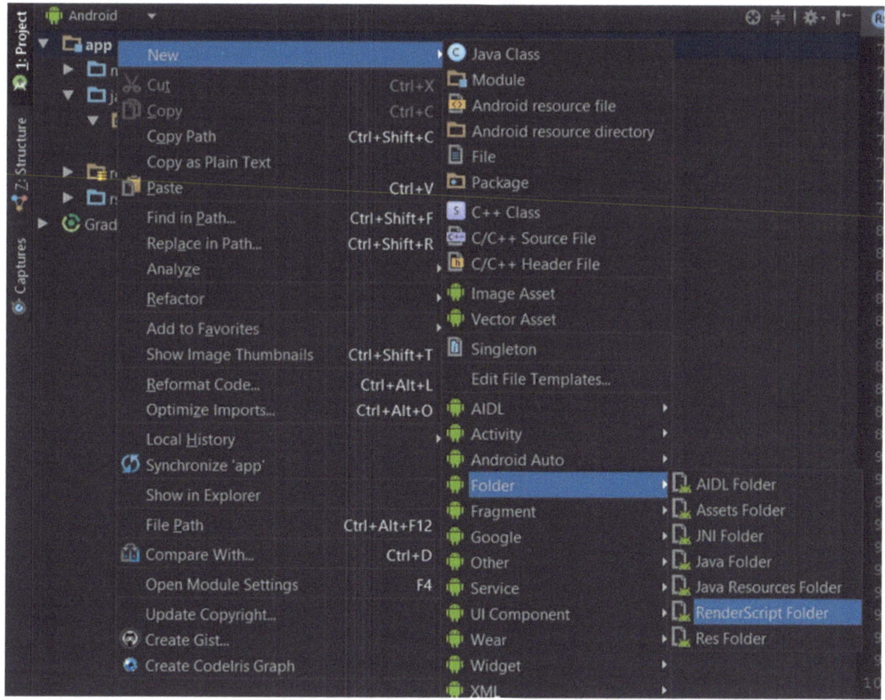

New RenderScript folder

Create an RS Script

Let's create an RS script named `sum.rs` inside the newly created `rs` folder, having the following content:

```c
// Needed directive for RS to work
#pragma version(1)

// Change java_package_name directive to match your Activity's package path
#pragma rs java_package_name(net.hydex11.firstexample)

// This kernel function will just sum 2 to every input element
// * in -> Current Allocation element
// * x  -> Current element index
int __attribute__((kernel)) sum2(int in, uint32_t x) {

    // Performs the sum and returns the new value
    return in + 2;

}
```

Java side

Note: remember that the default Java import for RenderScript is:

```java
import android.renderscript.*
```

Add a TextView to your Activity and set its `id` to debugTextView.

Edit your Activity's class, placing the following contents:

```java
@Override
protected void onCreate(Bundle savedInstanceState) {
    super.onCreate(savedInstanceState);
    setContentView(R.layout.activity_main);

    // Run the example
    example();
}

private void example() {

    // Instantiates the RenderScript context.
    RenderScript mRS = RenderScript.create(this);

    // Create an input array, containing some numbers.
    int inputArray[] = new int[]{0, 1, 2, 3, 4, 5, 6, 7, 8, 9};

    // Instantiates the input Allocation, that will contain our sample
    // numbers.
    Allocation inputAllocation = Allocation.createSized(mRS, Element.I32(mRS), inputArray.length);

    // Copies the input array into the input Allocation.
    inputAllocation.copyFrom(inputArray);

    // Instantiates the output Allocation, that will contain the result of the process.
    Allocation outputAllocation = Allocation.createSized(mRS,  Element.I32(mRS), inputArray.length);

    // Instantiates the sum script.
    ScriptC_sum myScript = new ScriptC_sum(mRS);

    // Run the sum process, taking the elements belonging to the inputAllocation and placing
```

```java
// the process results inside the outputAllocation.
myScript.forEach_sum2(inputAllocation, outputAllocation);

// Copies the result of the process from the outputAllocation to a simple int array.
int outputArray[] = new int[inputArray.length];
outputAllocation.copyTo(outputArray);

String debugString = "Output: ";
for (int i = 0; i < outputArray.length; i++)
    debugString += String.valueOf(outputArray[i]) + (i < outputArray.length - 1 ? ", " : "");

TextView textView = (TextView) findViewById(R.id.debugTextView);
textView.setText(debugString);

}
```

Run the code

Run the project and expect to see, in the TextView, the following string:

```
2, 3, 4, 5, 6, 7, 8, 9, 10, 11
```

Our input was:

```
0, 1, 2, 3, 4, 5, 6, 7, 8, 9
```

RenderScript iterated through the input Allocation and added 2 to every input element, storing the results inside the output Allocation.

Note: if you get the `cannot find symbol class ScriptC_sum` error, check that you edited your `java_package_name` to match your package correctly. Otherwise, Java will not be able to see your Script stub generated code.

Conclusions

In this chapter I provided a simple definition of RenderScript and a simple example to see it working. Now, to better understand the deep meaning of every RenderScript component, like what exactly is an **Element**, or how exactly an **Allocation** behaves, the next chapter is the right one.

RenderScript components

In this chapter I'll discuss RenderScript components, or **what makes RenderScript what it is**. Also, at the end of the chapter, I'll give an overview of the *RenderScript support library*.

The language

RenderScript is written in a C99[37]-like programming language and gets compiled using an llvm[38]-like compiler called slang[39].

RS language shares tons of traits with C99 and, as will be seen in this chapter, has some additions. Also, a notice is made for the following new elements:

> To check if the environment is 64-bit based, use the following preprocessor directive:

```
#ifdef __LP64__
```

For more information please refer to the *RenderScript and 64-bit* section.

> To check if the RS compile version (the one set using *renderscriptTargetApi* gradle setting) is greater/smaller than a specific one, use the following preprocessor directive:

```
#if (defined(RS_VERSION) && (RS_VERSION >= 14))
```

Element

A RenderScript element defines what kind of basic variable type the program is going to store in the memory. RS elements can be integers, floats, doubles, custom structs, etc..

There are two ways to declare an element:

> Use predefined RS elements, for example:
>> uchar (unsigned char) as `Element.U8(mRS)`
>> int as `Element.I32(mRS)`
>> packed float (4 elements) as `Element.F32_4(mRS)`
> Create your own element, by creating a struct[40] inside one of your scripts.

Predefined elements

A complete and up-to-date list of predefined elements can be found at the RenderScript value types reference page[41].

Basic elements are of two types:

1. Single value elements, like `int`, `float`, `double`.
2. Vector elements, like `int2`, `float2`, `double3`.

A single value integer maps, in Java side, to `Element.I32(mRS)`, while a vector one receives a suffix equal to the vector size (min 2, max 4), e.g. `Element.I32_3(mRS)`.

---

[37] C99 - Wikipedia - https://en.wikipedia.org/wiki/C99
[38] llvm.org - http://llvm.org/
[39] slang - RenderScript source code - https://android.googlesource.com/platform/frameworks/compile/slang/+/marshmallow-mr1-release/README.rst
[40] struct - Wikipedia - https://en.wikipedia.org/wiki/Struct_(C_programming_language)
[41] RenderScript value types reference page - Android developers - http://developer.android.com/guide/topics/renderscript/reference/rs_value_types.html

Inside RS scripts:

> Plain elements act as common vars: `int value = 3;`
> Packed elements act as struct elements (internally[42] defined using the ext_vector_type[43] attribute):

```
// Definition:
// typedef unsigned char uchar4 __attribute__((ext_vector_type(4)));

uchar4 myChar4;
myChar4.r = myChar4.x = myChar4.s0 = myChar4.S0;
myChar4.g = myChar4.y = myChar4.s1 = myChar4.S1;
myChar4.b = myChar4.z = myChar4.s2 = myChar4.S2;
myChar4.a = myChar4.w = myChar4.s3 = myChar4.S3;
```

Custom struct elements

RenderScript supports custom elements. To create one, declare a custom `typedef` struct like the following one, inside a script:

```
typedef struct MyElement {

    int x;
    int y;
    bool simpleBool;

} MyElement_t;
```

After the build process, a `ScriptField_MyElement` Java class will appear, mirroring the RS struct. You will be able to use this class to create a custom Allocation that uses your own Element:

```
// Declares a new Allocation, based upon the custom struct Element
Element myElement = ScriptField_MyElement.createElement(mRS);
Allocation myElementsAllocation = Allocation.createSized(mRS, myElement, 5);

// Or

Allocation myElementsAllocation = ScriptField_MyElement.create1D(mRS, sizeX).getAllocation();
```

You can find an example of this process inside the CustomElementExample sample project[44]. Also, inside the SurfaceRenderExample sample project[45] you can see how a custom element can be used to model a mathematical structure (in this case a particle, falling with some acceleration).

Inside RenderScript scripts:

> To get a custom element from an allocation:

```
MyElement_t el = * (MyElement_t *) rsGetElementAt(aIn, index);
```

> To set a custom element in an allocation:

```
rsSetElementAt(myAlloc, (void *)&el);
```

---

[42] RenderScript source code - `driver/rsdRuntimeStubs.cpp` -
https://android.googlesource.com/platform/frameworks/rs/+/marshmallow-mr1-release/driver/rsdRuntimeStubs.cpp#36
[43] ext_vector_type - llvm.org - http://clang.llvm.org/docs/LanguageExtensions.html#vectors-and-extended-vectors
[44] CustomElementExample sample project - https://bitbucket.org/cmaster11/rsbookexamples/src/tip/CustomElementExample/
[45] SurfaceRenderExample sample project - https://bitbucket.org/cmaster11/rsbookexamples/src/tip/SurfaceRenderExample/

Custom Java elements

You can create custom elements directly from the Java side, without defining the corresponding struct inside RenderScript, using `Element.Builder`.

Example:

```
Element.Builder eb = new Element.Builder(mRS);
eb.add(Element.I32(mRS), "x");
eb.add(Element.I32(mRS), "y");
eb.add(Element.F32(mRS), "fx");
eb.add(Element.F32(mRS), "fy");

Element myElement = eb.create();
```

You can find an example of this process inside the CustomJavaElementExample sample project[46].

Note: It is possible to use RenderScript auto generated code directly from the NDK side. However, custom structs are not yet supported (Android 23). Please refer to the *RenderScript NDK native support* section.

---

[46] CustomJavaElementExample sample project -
https://bitbucket.org/cmaster11/rsbookexamples/src/tip/CustomJavaElementExample/

Type

A RenderScript Type is the definition of the contents of an Allocation. It all starts with a `Type.Builder`. For the following examples, I'll be using:

```
RenderScript mRS;
Type.Builder tb;
Element.Builder eb;
Type mType;
Allocation mAlloc;
```

Example: I want to store a plain array of 54 integers

This initialization can be done in different ways:

> Using `Type.Builder`:

```
tb = new Type.Builder(mRS, Element.I32(mRS));
tb.setX(54);
mType = tb.create();
mAlloc = Allocation.createTyped(mRS, mType, Allocation.USAGE_SCRIPT);
```

> Using `Allocation.createSized`:

```
mAlloc = Allocation.createSized(mRS, Element.I32(mRS), 54);
```

Example: I want to store a 5-rows per 6-columns matrix of floats

To create multi dimensional Allocations, you need to use `Type.Builder`:

```
tb = new Type.Builder(mRS, Element.F32(mRS));
tb.setX(6);
tb.setY(5);
mType = tb.create();
mAlloc = Allocation.createTyped(mRS, mType, Allocation.USAGE_SCRIPT);
```

Example: I want to store an array of 5 custom Java elements, composed of 2 integers and 2 floats

Using the *previous example*:

```
Element.Builder eb = new Element.Builder(mRS);
eb.add(Element.I32(mRS), "x");
eb.add(Element.I32(mRS), "y");
eb.add(Element.F32(mRS), "fx");
eb.add(Element.F32(mRS), "fy");

// Define my element
Element myElement = eb.create();

tb = new Type.Builder(mRS, myElement);
tb.setX(5);
mType = tb.create();

mAlloc = Allocation.createTyped(mRS, mType, Allocation.USAGE_SCRIPT);

// OR, more straightforwardly
mAlloc = Allocation.createSized(mRS, myElement, 5);
```

Example: I want to store an array of 9 custom struct elements, composed of 2 integers and one bool

Using our aforementioned *custom struct element*.

```
// Declares a new Allocation, based upon the custom struct Element
Element myElement = ScriptField_MyElement.createElement(mRS);

tb = new Type.Builder(mRS, myElement);
tb.setX(9);
mType = tb.create();

mAlloc = Allocation.createTyped(mRS, mType, Allocation.USAGE_SCRIPT);

// OR, more straightforwardly
mAlloc = Allocation.createSized(mRS, myElement, 9);
```

Note: starting from Android API 21[47], it is possible to use methods like Type `createXY (..., int dimX, int dimY)` to instantiate a sized Type with ease.

Allocation

RenderScript Allocations behave like memory blocks, wherein bytes are sequentially ordered (the memory is contiguous, and indexing happens in a row-major[48] way, like it happens in plain C language).

For example, the following is an Allocation containing a 2-rows x 4-columns matrix of `int2` elements:

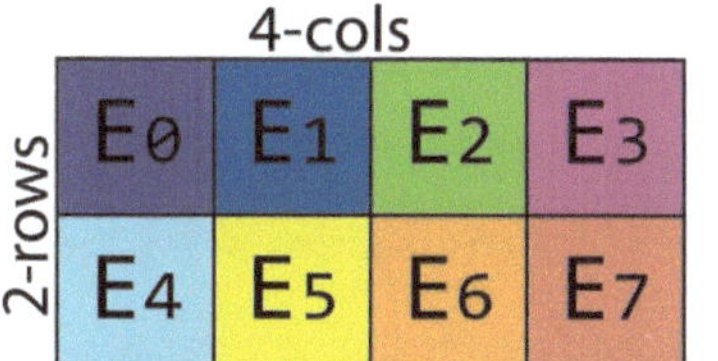

Memory order of 2D allocations' elements

RenderScript Allocations are a wrapper class, that have a memory pointer at their core created with a call to the RenderScript device-specific driver (`rsAllocation.cpp`[49]):

```
void* allocMem = rsc->mHal.funcs.allocRuntimeMem(sizeof(Allocation), 0);
if (!allocMem) {
    rsc->setError(RS_ERROR_FATAL_DRIVER, "Couldn't allocate memory for Allocation");
    return nullptr;
}
...
a = new (allocMem) Allocation(rsc, type, usages, mc, ptr);
```

Every operation applied to an Allocation directly modifies this memory block.

Allocations can be used inside an RS Script in at least three main ways:

> With a *kernel function*:

>> First, define the Allocation and fill it with data:

```
Allocation inAllocation = Allocation.createSized(mRS, Element.I32(mRS), 3);
```

>> Then, iterate through every element directly with a kernel function:

```
int __attribute__((kernel)) sum1(int in, uint32_t x) {
    return in + 1;
}
```

To invoke the kernel, the call on the Java side is:

```
script.forEach_sum1(inAllocation)
```

---

[48] Row-major order - Wikipedia - https://en.wikipedia.org/wiki/Row-major_order
[49] RenderScript source code - `rsAllocation.cpp` - https://android.googlesource.com/platform/frameworks/rs/+/marshmallow-mr1-release/rsAllocation.cpp#66

> With an `rs_allocation` variable:

  » Define an Allocation.
  » Create an `rs_allocation` variable inside one of your RS Scripts:

```
rs_allocation aIn;
```

  » Bind it to the Java side, using:

```
myScript.set_aIn(myAllocation);
```

  » Access that allocation using `rsGetElementAt` and `rsSetElementAt` functions sets (inside a kernel or inside simple functions):

    » If you want to retrieve an integer:

```
int var = rsGetElementAt_int(aIn, index);
```

    » If you want to retrieve an integer vector:

```
int3 var = rsGetElementAt_int3(aIn, index);
```

    » If you want to retrieve a custom struct element:

```
MyElement_t el = * (MyElement_t *) rsGetElementAt(aIn, index);
```

    » If you want to set a float in a matrix:

```
rsSetElementAt_float(aIn, newValue, x, y);
```

> With a **pointer**:

  » Define a 1-dimensional Allocation (it is not possible to use multi dimensional arrays with pointers, when compiling the project using API 20 and higher[50]).
  » Create, inside a RenderScript Script, a pointer that resembles your Allocation base Element:

```
int * myIntAllocationPtr;
uchar * myUCharAllocationPtr;
```

Note: it is not suitable to try to use custom Java Elements with a pointer, because void `*` `ptr;` doesn't get reflected onto the Java side.

  » Access your pointer with memory offsets:

    E.g. I want to retrieve the 12th element of my Allocation:

```
int element = myIntAllocationPtr[11];
```

---

[50] Android source code - `renderscript/Script.java` -
https://android.googlesource.com/platform/frameworks/base/+/marshmallow-release/rs/java/android/renderscript/Script.java#312

Allocations can have different usages:

- › Script access (default), `Allocation.USAGE_SCRIPT`.
- › Bitmap shared access, `Allocation.USAGE_SHARED`, will use the already existing native memory of a Bitmap, instead of copying its content in the Allocation. This usage is automatically implemented when using the `createFromBitmap` function:

```
// Inside Allocation.java code, when calling createFromBitmap()
return createFromBitmap(rs, b, MipmapControl.MIPMAP_NONE, USAGE_SHARED | USAGE_SCRIPT
                                                  | USAGE_GRAPHICS_TEXTURE);
```

- › Graphics texture, `Allocation.USAGE_GRAPHICS_TEXTURE`, which is a non mutable storage.
- › IO input/output, `Allocation.USAGE_IO_INPUT`/`Allocation.USAGE_IO_OUTPUT`, which is used to interface the Allocation with a Surface.

For a complete list of usage types, please refer to the RenderScript Allocation reference page[51].

Note: when an Allocation gets declared, its content is undefined, so it must be initialized before using it (do not expect it to be filled with 0).

It is possible to access Allocations directly from the NDK side. To see an example of that process, please refer to the *Native Allocation access* chapter.

---

[51] RenderScript Allocation reference page - http://developer.android.com/reference/android/renderscript/Allocation.html

Context

Everything starts with a Context. It is used to establish a binding between RenderScript and the running Activity/Application. Whatever element is bound to an RS Context will be able to interact with all other RS elements: this means that you will be able to access different elements from different parts of the context.

The simplest scenario is:

> Take two RS scripts, each one having an `rs_allocation` variable.
> From Java, call `script.set_variableName(Allocation)` on each script, and pass the same Allocation Java variable.
> Both scripts will be able to read and write the same Allocation.

RS Context is declared with:

```
RenderScript mRS = RenderScript.create((Context) activityInstance);
```

Debug note

It is possible to enable a debug mode by instantiating the context with the following line:

```
RenderScript mRS = RenderScript.create((Context) activityInstance, RenderScript.ContextType.DEBUG);

// OR, to debug RS if BuildConfig is DEBUG

RenderScript mRS = RenderScript.create(MainActivity.this, BuildConfig.DEBUG
                                              ? RenderScript.ContextType.DEBUG
                                              : RenderScript.ContextType.NORMAL);
```

While operating in this mode, more checks will be performed during the execution of the code. For example, the following error can appear if you try to set an element out of its bounds (trying to set element at index 300 when the maximum would be 285, the vector being 286 elements long):

```
android.renderscript.RSRuntimeException: Fatal error 2048, details:
                        Out range ElementAt X 300 of 286 at
                        android.renderscript.RenderScript$MessageThread.run(RenderScript.java)
Error from void SC_SetElementAt1_uchar4(
                        android::renderscript::rs_allocation, const uchar4 *, uint32_t)
```

Note: the debug mode makes RenderScript perform slower and should only be used for developing purposes.

Script

RenderScript scripts are files with `.rs` extension. Scripts can use different preprocessor directives:

> `pragma version(1)`, which is **required** for every script.
> `#pragma rs java_package_name(com.example)`, **required**, which defines the Java package under which the reflected code will be generated.
> `#pragma rs_fp_full`, set by default, enables full IEEE 754-2008 standard[52] support.
> `#pragma rs_fp_relaxed`, which disables support for denormalized numbers[53]: numbers too small turn simply to zero. This process is done usually when dealing with SSE extensions[54] and provides faster calculations (of course with less precision).
> `#pragma rs_fp_imprecise`, which is deprecated[55] and, if used, behaves as `rs_fp_relaxed`.
> `#include "myHeader.rsh"`, to include other files.

`#pragma rs_fp_relaxed`

`rs_fp_relaxed` lets RenderScript achieve the **best** performance. Embedded math functions (like mad[56]) benefit from this pragma in terms of speed (of course there is a trade-off between speed and precision).

As stated in `cpu_ref/rsCpuScript.cpp`[57] RS source code file, `rs_fp_relaxed` can enable NEON instructions[58] for math script-functions, which provide a huge performance boost:

```
#if defined(ARCH_ARM_HAVE_NEON) && !defined(DISABLE_CLCORE_NEON)
    enum bcinfo::RSFloatPrecision prec = ME.getRSFloatPrecision();
    if (prec == bcinfo::RS_FP_Relaxed) {
        // NEON-capable ARMv7a devices can use an accelerated math library
        // for all reduced precision scripts.
        // ARMv8 does not use NEON, as ASIMD can be used with all precision
        // levels.
        return SYSLIBPATH"/libclcore_neon.bc";
    } else {
        return defaultLib;
    }
#elif defined(__i386__) || defined(__x86_64__)
    // x86 devices will use an optimized library.
    return SYSLIBPATH"/libclcore_x86.bc";
#else
    return defaultLib;
#endif
```

Note: `rs_fp_relaxed` can cause problems on Adreno GPUs if, inside scripts that use the pragma, multidimensional static arrays are used.

An error can be:

```
<rsdQueryGlobals:990>: ERROR: Address not found for myVariableName
<rsdVendorScriptInitQCOM:783>: ERROR: rsdQueryGlobals returned -30
```

Where (for example) `myVariableName` is `static int myVariableName[5][3];`

---

[52] IEEE 754-2008 standard - https://standards.ieee.org/findstds/standard/754-2008.html
[53] Denormalized numbers - Wikipedia - https://en.wikipedia.org/wiki/Denormal_number
[54] SSE extensions - Wikipedia - https://en.wikipedia.org/wiki/Streaming_SIMD_Extensions
[55] slang source code - `slang_rs_pragma_handler.cpp` -
https://android.googlesource.com/platform/frameworks/compile/slang/+/marshmallow-release/slang_rs_pragma_handler.cpp#186
[56] RenderScript source code - `api/rs_math.spec` - https://android.googlesource.com/platform/frameworks/rs/+/marshmallow-mr1-release/api/rs_math.spec#960
[57] RenderScript source code - `cpu_ref/rsCpuScript.cpp` -
https://android.googlesource.com/platform/frameworks/rs/+/marshmallow-mr1-release/cpu_ref/rsCpuScript.cpp#477
[58] NEON instructions - http://www.arm.com/products/processors/technologies/neon.php

If this error appears, the entire script **will not behave in the right way**.

Script components

Inside RS scripts you can find different basic elements, like:

> `init` function.
> Variables.
> Non-static functions.
> Static functions.
> Kernel functions.

Note: being written in a C99-derived language, RS script functions accept the `__attribute__`[59] keyword (also available for variables' attributes[60] and types' attributes[61]), with a custom implementation:

> `__attribute__((kernel))` will declare a kernel function and force a compile-time check of its attributes (`RSExportForEach::validateAndConstructKernelParams` function[62]), for example (not complete list):
>> Must be used on API level >= 17.
>> Cannot return a pointer.
>> Cannot have pointer-like input arguments.

Init function

It is possible to declare an `init` function, that gets executed automatically on a Script's initialization. It may be used, for example, to initialize static complex variables at runtime.

A basic declaration of it is as follows:

```
void init(){
    // init code here :)
}
```

Variables

RS scripts' variables can be static or not. A non-static variable (`int myVar`) can be accessed from the Java side **only to set its value, not to retrieve it**. It is possible to retrieve only the compile-time values directly (which turn into a Java constant):

```
int var = 3;

// Inside some func
var++;
```

Then called from Java, this will always return 3:

```
myScript.get_var() == 3 // Use myScript.set_var(value) to set the value
```

Static variables can be accessed only from inside an RS script. Common use is to have them behave as counters:

```
static int myCounter = 0;

// Inside kernel
rsAtomicInc(&myCounter); // Increments by 1 the value
rsAtomicAdd(&myCounter, 3); // Increments by 3 the value
```

---

[59] GCC - `__attribute__` keyword - https://gcc.gnu.org/onlinedocs/gcc/Function-Attributes.html#Function-Attributes
[60] GCC - variables' attributes - https://gcc.gnu.org/onlinedocs/gcc/Common-Variable-Attributes.html#Common-Variable-Attributes
[61] GCC - types' attributes - https://gcc.gnu.org/onlinedocs/gcc/Common-Type-Attributes.html#Common-Type-Attributes
[62] slang source code - `slang_rs_export_foreach.cpp` - `RSExportForEach::validateAndConstructKernelParams` function - https://android.googlesource.com/platform/frameworks/compile/slang/+/marshmallow-mr1-release/slang_rs_export_foreach.cpp#208

Using atomic functions is needed inside kernel functions to preserve memory consistency. For a complete list of atomic functions, please refer to the RenderScript Atomic Update Functions page[63]. **Note:** atomic functions can be used even on non-static variables.

Note: you should always initialize script variables, static or not, as otherwise you may incur in a SIGSEGV error, like the following one:

```
A/libc: Fatal signal 11 (SIGSEGV), code 1, fault addr 0x58 in tid 29099
```

Non-static functions

Inside RS scripts it is possible to define functions that can be called from the Java side:

```
int myVal = 0;

// Only void return type is accepted
void setVal(int value){ myVal = value; }
```

Call from Java with `myScript.invoke_setVal(value)`.

Non static functions cannot have a return value.

Static functions

Inside RS scripts it is possible to define **static functions**:

```
static int getNum(){ return 3; }
```

These kinds of functions are not mapped to Java and can have a return value. These functions can be used as normal C functions.

Kernel

RenderScript kernel functions are used to iterate through Allocation elements and perform operations onto them.

Kernel functions operate on input and output Allocations (at least one input or one output Allocation):

> One input:

```
void __attribute__((kernel)) kernelFunctionName(float in, uint32_t x){ ... }

// OR
// Pointer v_in refers to current input element
void kernelFunctionName(const uchar4 * v_in, uint32_t x){ ... }
```

Call it with:

```
script.forEach_kernelFunctionName(inAllocation);
```

> One output:

```
double __attribute__((kernel)) kernelFunctionName(uint32_t x){ ... }

// OR
// Pointer v_out refers to current output element
void kernelFunctionName(float * v_out, uint32_t x){ ... }
```

Call it with:

```
script.forEach_kernelFunctionName(outAllocation);
```

---

[63] RenderScript Atomic Update Functions page - http://developer.android.com/guide/topics/renderscript/reference/rs_atomic.html

> One input and one output:

```
int2 __attribute__((kernel)) kernelFunctionName(float in, uint32_t x, uint32_t y){ ... }

// OR
// Pointer v_in refers to current input element and v_out refers to current output element
void kernelFunctionName(const uchar2 * v_in, float * v_out, uint32_t x, uint32_t y){ ... }
```

Call it with:

```
script.forEach_kernelFunctionName(inAllocation, outAllocation);
```

Note: input and output Allocations need to have the same X, Y, Z dimensions (**the base Element can differ**).

Note: starting from API 21 it is possible to use the RS_KERNEL[64] flag, instead of using the __attribute__((kernel)) one, to declare a kernel function.

Note: different ways to access Allocations' elements offer different performances. To better understand their impact, please refer to the *Performance notes* chapter.

Note: kernels' indexing arguments, like x and y, must be of the same type and the type must be one between: int, uint, int32_t and uint32_t. This constraint can be seen in the slang_rs_export_foreach.cpp[65] *slang compiler* source file.

Function - rsForEach

It is possible to call a kernel directly from inside an RS script, using the rsForEach function.

Note: The usage of this function lets you provide the kernel with some custom user data, which can be sent even using the RenderScript.forEach() function on the Java side to perform the same task. Inside the KernelUserDataExample sample project[66], you can find an implementation of both methods.

To make the call possible, at least the following three elements have to be defined:

> Kernel to be executed (must be a simple, non-static function called root):

```
// Iterates through float2-based Allocations.
// usrData contains custom data, which user passes to the kernel (optional)
void root(const float2 *in, float2 *out, const void *usrData, uint32_t x, uint32_t y){ ... }
```

> An RS function to call the kernel:

```
void runScriptKernel(rs_script myScript, rs_allocation in_alloc, rs_allocation out_alloc)
{

    // Custom user variable
    int userVariable = 5;

    // Calls kernel function root of script myScript
    rsForEach(myScript, in_alloc, out_alloc, &userVariable, sizeof(int));

}
```

> A Java call to runScriptKernel function:

```
myScript.invoke_runScriptKernel(myScript, inputAllocation, outputAllocation);
```

---

[64] RenderScript source code - api/rs_core.spec - https://android.googlesource.com/platform/frameworks/rs/+/marshmallow-mr1-release/api/rs_core.spec#34
[65] slang source code - slang_rs_export_foreach.cpp - https://android.googlesource.com/platform/frameworks/compile/slang/+/marshmallow-mr1-release/slang_rs_export_foreach.cpp#374
[66] KernelUserDataExample sample project - https://bitbucket.org/cmaster11/rsbookexamples/src/tip/KernelUserDataExample/

Inside the `scriptc/rs_for_each.rsh`[67] Android source file it is possible to find all definitions of `rsForEach` function:

```c
#if (defined(RS_VERSION) && (RS_VERSION >= 14) && (RS_VERSION <= 20))
extern void __attribute__((overloadable)) rsForEach(rs_script script,
                           rs_allocation input, rs_allocation output, const void* usrData,
                                        size_t usrDataLen, const rs_script_call_t* sc);
#endif
#if (defined(RS_VERSION) && (RS_VERSION >= 14) && (RS_VERSION <= 20))
extern void __attribute__((overloadable)) rsForEach(rs_script script,
                                          rs_allocation input, rs_allocation output,
                                          const void* usrData, size_t usrDataLen);
#endif

#if (defined(RS_VERSION) && (RS_VERSION >= 14))
extern void __attribute__((overloadable))
    rsForEach(rs_script script, rs_allocation input, rs_allocation output);
#endif
```

As can be seen, until RenderScript target API 20, it is possible to use custom user data and run limits (as discussed below) from inside RS scripts, while afterwards its usage got deprecated.

Kernel run limits

The first `rsForEach` definition contains a reference to `rs_script_call_t` struct, defined as:

```c
typedef struct rs_script_call {
    enum rs_for_each_strategy strategy;
    uint32_t xStart;
    uint32_t xEnd;
    uint32_t yStart;
    uint32_t yEnd;
    uint32_t zStart;
    uint32_t zEnd;
    uint32_t arrayStart;
    uint32_t arrayEnd;
} rs_script_call_t;
```

It is possible to use this `struct` to limit a kernel execution, both from the Java and RS sides:

> From the RS side, you can define an instance of `rs_script_call_t` and call a kernel that uses it:

```c
    rs_script myScript; // Given as input
    rs_allocation in_alloc; // Given as input
    rs_allocation out_alloc; // Given as input

    rs_script_call_t kernelCallLimits;

    // Limits are EXCLUSIVE
    int myXLimit = 234; // Will iterate until index 233
    int myYLimit = 10;

    // Refer to enum rs_for_each_strategy, but do not expect this setting
    // to be respected from every system (you are doing parallel computing!)
    kernelCallLimits.strategy = RS_FOR_EACH_STRATEGY_DONT_CARE;

    kernelCallLimits.xStart = 0;
    kernelCallLimits.xEnd = myXLimit;
    kernelCallLimits.yStart = 0;
```

---

[67] RenderScript source code - `scriptc/rs_for_each.rsh` -
https://android.googlesource.com/platform/frameworks/rs/+/marshmallow-mr1-release/scriptc/rs_for_each.rsh

```c
kernelCallLimits.yEnd = myYLimit;
kernelCallLimits.zStart = 0;
kernelCallLimits.zEnd = 0;
kernelCallLimits.arrayStart = 0;
kernelCallLimits.arrayEnd = 0;

rsForEach(myScript, in_alloc, out_alloc, NULL, 0, &kernelCallLimits);

// Or, if you have custom data
rsForEach(myScript, in_alloc, out_alloc, &myCustomData, sizeof(myCustomData), &kernelCallLimits);
```

> From the Java side, using the LaunchOptions class:

```java
Script.LaunchOptions launchOptions = new Script.LaunchOptions();

// Limits are EXCLUSIVE
int myXLimit = 234;
int myYLimit = 10;

launchOptions.setX(0, myXLimit);
launchOptions.setX(0, myYLimit);
myScript.forEach_myKernelName(inputAllocation, outputAllocation, launchOptions);
```

Asynchronism note

RenderScript kernels and the Java side run in an asynchronous way. Multiple Java `forEach` calls will create an RS call queue, so that kernels will run synchronously inside their RS context (as shown in the image below). When the `mRS.finish()` function gets called, it will wait for the call queue to end (like `std::thread::join`[68] function does in C++).

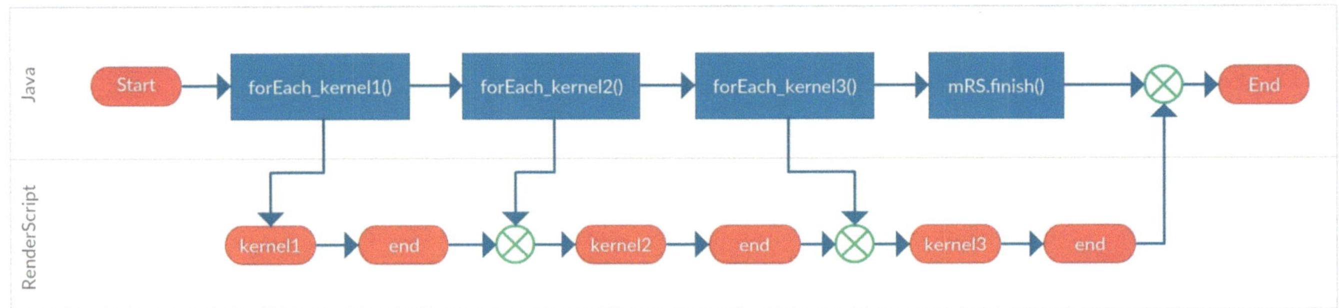

Asynchronous RenderScript kernels execution

Parallel processing note

As a general parallel processing argument, it is always better to operate on a **large** number of elements than on few.

Let's take for example the process of visual features extraction[69]. Sometimes it is required to generate a "pyramid" of scaled images, starting from a source one. This pyramid is generated cyclically and images are stored in a vector (one scaled image is a vector element). One common performance related mistake is the following:

```java
ArrayList<Allocation> mAllocArray; // Contains one Allocation per image

for (int i = 0; i < numImage; i++)
{
    myScript.forEach_myKernel(mAllocArray.get(i));
}
```

This operation is going to take much more time than executing the `myKernel` function over a single big image.

---

[68] `std::thread::join` - cppreference.com - http://en.cppreference.com/w/cpp/thread/thread/join
[69] Feature extraction - Wikipedia - https://en.wikipedia.org/wiki/Feature_extraction

Using parallel computing paradigms, the fastest approach is to use a single, big image, stored in a single Allocation, as shown in the following image:

Difference between vector-style and bundle-style approaches

Example of composed pyramid:

Bundle pyramid example: elements are ordered to take up as less space as possible

Note: You can find an example of this concept inside the LargeSetExample sample project[70]. The example performs calculations using two different scenarios:

> A vector of input allocations, having a size that decreases linearly (for example, if the first allocation has a size of 100 elements, the second one will have a size of 83 elements and so on), like what happens in the above image.
> A single allocation, whose size is the sum of the size of all vector allocations.

By running the example, a common result (on a Samsung Galaxy Note 3) is the following:

```
I/Timings: Single allocation execution: 84.804ms
I/Timings: Vector allocations execution: 557.976ms
```

---

[70] LargeSetExample sample project - https://bitbucket.org/cmaster11/rsbookexamples/src/tip/LargeSetExample/

FilterScript

FilterScript is a subset of RenderScript, optimized for pure GPU usage. It's possible to define a FS script just by using the `.fs` extension.

Using FS implies `#pragma rs_fp_relaxed` flag, so do not declare it as it would trigger a compile error.

FilterScript has some limitations (its speed depends on them):

> It is not possible to use pointers (for example, `int * myAllocation`). The only acceptable usage is when dealing with custom Elements Allocations:

```
rs_allocation myAlloc;

// Generic function, can be a kernel
void ...(){
    // Get element
    MyElement_t el = *(MyElement_t*)(rsGetElementAt(myAlloc, index));
    // Set element
    rsSetElementAt(myAlloc, (void *)&el);
}
```

> Static variables cannot be used. As seen with Qualcomm Adreno drivers (GPU family with big market share[71], 2015/12), there are many bitcode compile errors when using static variables. Their usage is therefore discouraged.

The drawback of this problem is that it is not possible to use multidimensional arrays:

```
// This declaration is invalid because slang compiler doesn't know how to reflect it on the Java
// side, so fails compiling.
int myArray[M][N];

// This declaration prevents FilterScript from working on Adreno GPUs
static int myArray[M][N];
```

> It's not possible to use 64-bit values, so it's not possible to use double and long types.

FilterScript gives a performance boost when operating on devices having a decent GPU and respective device-specific RenderScript driver. Otherwise, its performance is just comparable to standard RenderScript implementation. Also, FilterScript offers good performance when reading multiple elements from the same kernel function, if compared to the standard RS. For more information about this concept, please refer to the *Performance notes* chapter.

Message queue

It's possible to have RenderScript communicate with Java using a message queue.

On the Java side, it's possible to instantiate a RSMessageHandler class that will receive messages sent from the RS side:

> Create an RSMessageHandler instance:

```java
static final int MESSAGE_OK = 1;

RenderScript.RSMessageHandler myHandler = new RenderScript.RSMessageHandler(){
    @Override
    public void run()
    {
        switch (mID)
        {
            case MESSAGE_OK: // Or ScriptC_myScript.const_MESSAGE_OK
            {
                // mData (int[]) contains sent data (if any).
                int x = mData[0];
                // The usage of intBitsToFloat, to cast integer to float, is necessary
                float f = Float.intBitsToFloat(mData[1]);
            }
            break;
            default: super.run();
                break;
        }
    }
};
```

> Set the handler instance to handle messages:

```java
mRS.setMessageHandler(myHandler);
```

> On the RS side, send data to the Java one:

```c
const int MESSAGE_OK = 1;

// Inside function/kernel
struct {
    int x;
    float f;
} data;

data.x = 5;
data.f = 1.3f;

// Sends struct data to the Java side
rsSendToClient(MESSAGE_OK, (void*)&data, sizeof(data));

// Or, if the send function has to be blocking (you want it to wait for its message to be sent to
// the queue before proceeding):
rsSendToClientBlocking(MESSAGE_OK, (void*)&data, sizeof(data));
```

To see a working example, please take a look at our RSMessageHandlerExample sample project[72]

---

[72] RSMessageHandlerExample sample project -
https://bitbucket.org/cmaster11/rsbookexamples/src/tip/RSMessageHandlerExample/

Note: this method is **slow** for real-time purposes. It is faster to use an Allocation as a buffer instead of using message queues.

RenderScript support library

In case you want to target older Android APIs (API < 18), please use the Android Support Library v8[73]. To enable it add, together with the previous definitions, the following:

```
renderscriptSupportModeEnabled true
```

Also, you can then lower `renderscriptTargetApi` and `minSdkVersion` (they must have the same value) to match a lower Android API version (the minimum you can use is Android API 8).

Inside your Java classes, you will need to import the following package, instead of using the `import android.renderscript.*` directive:

```
import android.support.v8.renderscript.*;
```

You can look at this support library's source code inside Android source code repository[74].

USAGE_IO flags

The Android support library v8 did not support `USAGE_IO_INPUT` or `USAGE_IO_OUTPUT` flags until the API 23 release, where `libRSSupportIO.so` was introduced inside the SDK prebuilts section[75]. A custom wrapper library is provided, RSSupportIOWrapper[76], which is used inside the SurfaceRenderExample sample project[77] sample project. This library embeds the latest `libRSSupportIO.so` shared library, to enable support fot these flags.

The need of creating such a wrapper was born because, at the time of writing this book, Android SDK Build Tools 23.0.2[78] did not offer `libRSSupportIO.so` support library.

Book note

In this book, the support library gets used inside the SurfaceRenderExample sample project[79], which shows both the standard setup for it and support for the custom RSSupportIOWrapper[80].

Conclusions

In this chapter I offered a broad overview about RenderScript main components:

> Element: defines what an Allocation is made of.
> Type: defines an Allocation size.
> Allocation: stores data that Kernel functions access.
> Kernel: executes operations on Allocations' data.
> Context: wraps the entire RenderScript system status.
> Script: defines the RS computational logic.

The main component, on which the entire structure relies, is the **Kernel** function. Its performance is a big topic, and I'm covering it in the following chapter.

---

[73] Android Support Library v8 - http://developer.android.com/tools/support-library/features.html#v8
[74] Android source code repository - https://android.googlesource.com/platform/frameworks/support.git/+/marshmallow-release/v8/renderscript/java/src/android/support/v8/renderscript
[75] SDK prebuilts section - https://android.googlesource.com/platform/prebuilts/sdk/+/marshmallow-release/renderscript/lib/arm/
[76] RSSupportIOWrapper - https://bitbucket.org/cmaster11/mrssupportiowrapper
[77] SurfaceRenderExample sample project - https://bitbucket.org/cmaster11/rsbookexamples/src/tip/SurfaceRenderExample/
[78] Android SDK Build Tools 23.0.2 - http://developer.android.com/tools/revisions/build-tools.html
[79] SurfaceRenderExample sample project - https://bitbucket.org/cmaster11/rsbookexamples/src/tip/SurfaceRenderExample/
[80] RSSupportIOWrapper - https://bitbucket.org/cmaster11/mrssupportiowrapper

Performance notes

Performance is a topic that would require tons of different discussions. Therefore, only the following relevant topics will be presented here:

> Memory access cost
> Pure calculation cost

One relevant notice is that performance is totally dependent upon the RenderScript driver. The driver is usually provided by chipset developers (e.g. Qualcomm for Adreno GPUs, ARM for Mali GPUs). To understand how it works, please refer to the *RenderScript driver* section.

Memory architecture

One noticeable difference between doing parallel computing with RenderScript and other desktop systems (e.g. CUDA[81]) is the different architecture the system relies on:

> Mobile phones offer a shared memory[82] architecture, where CPU and GPU share the same address space.
> Desktop GPUs have a dedicated memory, which gets used to store relevant graphics data (e.g. textures).

This difference defines a limit for mobile phones: the benefit achieved using parallel computing on shared memory architectures exists only when there is a good balance between pure calculation and memory access. It is not always comfortable to directly use existing algorithms made, for example, for the CUDA environment, if they rely heavily on GPU memory access speed. What must be reminded is that GPU-based computing should be used in throughput-critical applications (where large amounts of data have to be processed all together), while CPU-based computing should be used in latency-critical ones[83] (where very fast calculations are needed).

To better understand the difference between desktop and mobile environments, let's take a look at a numerical comparison between high-end devices:

Environment	Device	Kind	Release date	Memory bandwidth (GB/s)
Mobile	Samsung Galaxy S6	CPU+GPU	March, 2015	24.88[84] (shared memory)
Desktop	Haswell-E	CPU architecture	Q3'14	~70[85]
Desktop	GeForce GTX 980	GPU	September, 2014	224[86]

When using desktop GPUs it is possible to take advantage of the memory speed factor (e.g. 3x), but when using mobile phones this benefit disappears. Reducing the number of accesses when possible is mandatory to achieve good performance using RenderScript (and, more generally, when doing parallel computing on mobile devices).

Example: convolution

One common operation done with image analysis is convolution[87]: a kernel function operates on a central pixel and extracts information from neighbor ones to compute the final value of its central one. Blurring, edge detection and

---

[81] CUDA - NVIDIA - http://www.nvidia.com/object/cuda_home_new.html
[82] Shared memory - Wikipedia - https://en.wikipedia.org/wiki/Shared_memory
[83] Sparsh Mittal, Jeffrey S. Vetter - A Survey of CPU-GPU Heterogeneous Computing Techniques - https://www.academia.edu/12355899/A_Survey_of_CPU-GPU_Heterogeneous_Computing_Techniques
[84] AnandTech - The Samsung Galaxy S6 and S6 edge Review - http://www.anandtech.com/show/9146/the-samsung-galaxy-s6-and-s6-edge-review/2
[85] Corsair - DDR3 vs. DDR4: Four Generations, Raw Bandwidth by the Numbers - http://www.corsair.com/en-us/blog/2015/september/ddr3_vs_ddr4_generational
[86] NVIDIA - GeForce GTX 980 specifications - http://www.geforce.com/hardware/desktop-gpus/geforce-gtx-980/specifications
[87] Convolution - Wikipedia - https://en.wikipedia.org/wiki/Convolution

sharpening[88] are operations made using the convolution process. Convolution's computational cost is linearly related to the total number of accessed elements, and the access cost formula is as follows:

```
cost(radius) = (radius * 2 + 1)^2
```

Such kind of algorithm is proportionally slower (the bigger the radius, the slower the algorithm) on mobile phone architectures than on desktop ones, because of the memory access cost.

GPU or CPU?

Algorithms that need to access a broad amount of sparse elements might me more suitable to be run directly on CPU. When doing parallel computing on desktop systems, the best performance is achieved when both GPU and CPU are stressed and busy. On mobile phones however, system reactivity is a fundamental matter (the user must always feel that the system is responsive to enjoy its experience): this is why stressing the GPU, instead of the CPU, can be a good way to keep the system's response speed high.

Note: Android's UI is hardware accelerated[89], so, the aforementioned argument is valid only until a certain degree. Filling the 100% of GPU's usage is never recommended, but keep in mind that the CPU is vital for the entire mobile system, and occupying it at the maximum degree brings serious problems to the whole environment.

A noticeable benchmark for a "suggested CPU and GPU usage" situation can be found in the *FAST features detection* chapter.

---

[88] Blurring, edge detection and sharpening - Wikipedia - https://en.wikipedia.org/wiki/Kernel_(image_processing)
[89] Android Developers - Hardware Acceleration - http://developer.android.com/guide/topics/graphics/hardware-accel.html

Profiler sample project

I created a sample project, ProfilerExample[90], to study how RenderScript performance differs among different devices. The project, at the moment of writing this book, analyzes the following topics:

> Memory access, read and write operations.
> Pure calculation functions.
> Multiple kernels call sequences.

Profiler: memory access

Memory access performance can be evaluated by analyzing write and read operations cost. Examples of read and write operations are as follows:

> **Blurring**, that computes the average of an **n-per-n** square surrounding a pixel: its main computation is accessing neighbor elements and performing calculations.
> **Setting output values** over a square-shaped area: its main operation is writing to memory.
> **RGBA to grayscale conversion**: its main computation is a pure calculation, whose output gets placed on an Allocation having a different base Element (uchar4 to uchar).

Note: radius-based tests are run with the following radiuses: 1, 3 and 5.

Kernel functions

For every tested task, at most the following kernel functions are tested (each kernel function performs the same calculations for the same task), each iterating over a source bitmap having a size of 500x286 pixels:

> Simple kernel function (uses `rsGetElementAt` to retrieve input elements):

```
uchar4 __attribute__((kernel)) simpleKernel(uint32_t x, uint32_t y){ ... }
```

> *FilterScript* implementation of simple kernel function (uses `rsGetElementAt` to retrieve input elements):

```
uchar4 __attribute__((kernel)) simpleKernelFS(uint32_t x, uint32_t y){ ... }
```

> Pointer-based in/out kernel function:

```
void pointerKernel(const uchar4 * v_in, uchar4 * v_out, uint32_t x, uint32_t y){ ... }
```

> Pointer-based in kernel function (uses `rsSetElementAt` to set output elements):

```
void pointerKernelSet(const uchar4 * v_in, uint32_t x, uint32_t y){ ... }
```

> Pointer-based out kernel function (uses `rsGetElementAt` to set input elements):

```
void pointerKernelGet(uchar4 * v_out, uint32_t x, uint32_t y){ ... }
```

> In-script allocated variable kernel functions, which use, as input, an array directly loaded inside the script's context:

```
// Test an allocation directly loaded inside a script
const int pngWidth = 500;
const int pngHeight = 286;
uchar4 pngData[pngWidth * pngHeight];

// Kernel function used to load image data
void __attribute__((kernel)) fillPngData(uchar4 in, uint32_t x, uint32_t y){
    pngData[x + y * pngWidth] = in;
}
```

» Pointer-based out kernel function

```
void pointerKernelGetFromScriptVariable(uchar4 * v_out, uint32_t x, uint32_t y){ ... }
```

» Pointer-based out kernel function, which uses, as input, the pointer to the array directly loaded inside the script's context:

```
void pointerKernelGetFromScriptVariablePointer(uchar4 * v_out, uint32_t x, uint32_t y){ ... }
```

» FilterScript implementation of simple kernel function:

```
uchar4 __attribute__((kernel)) simpleKernelFSGetFromScriptVariable(uint32_t x, uint32_t y)
                                                                                   { ... }
```

> Pointer-based NDK implementation. Iterates through every needed element and uses the OpenMP[91] parallelization library.

Profiler: pure calculation

A standard way to stress CPUs is calculating PI digits, as seen in software like Super PI[92] and y-cruncher[93].

In the profiler, the Nilakantha's Series[94] is implemented. It is run with four different iteration counts (1500, 3000, 6000 and 12000), each iterating over allocations made of 128 elements.

Implemented tests are:

> PI calculation, RenderScript implementation.
> PI calculation, FilterScript implementation.
> PI calculation, NDK side implementation.

Profiler: kernels calling

As seen in the *kernel* paragraph, it is possible to invoke kernel functions using different approaches. In the profiler, the following test cases are implemented, each iterating on 262144 elements:

> Invoking two kernels (A and B), sequentially, directly from the Java side.
> Invoking two kernels (A and B), sequentially, using `rsForEach` script-function.
> Invoking a single kernel (A + B), directly from the Java side.
> Invoking a single kernel (A + B), using `rsForEach` script-function.

Test specifics

Total samples count per device must be high, for example higher than 15000. A big number of cycles is chosen because testing made on Android smartphones can have a big variance[95] in its results (this happens, for example, when background tasks perform calculations, interfering with the foreground ones). Given the variance possible problem, the harmonic mean[96] is used to calculate the average computing time of kernel functions. Its calculation makes outliers[97] count less in the final value. The standard situation in profiling code on Android can be represented by the following sample data:

```
Values
    4    5    3    6    3    5    30   4    6    6    25   3
```

---

[91] OpenMP - http://openmp.org/wp/
[92] Super PI - http://www.superpi.net/
[93] y-cruncher - numberworld.org - http://www.numberworld.org/y-cruncher/
[94] Nilakantha's Series - CodeProject - http://www.codeproject.com/Articles/813185/Calculating-the-Number-PI-Through-Infinite-Sequenc
[95] Variance - Wikipedia - https://en.wikipedia.org/wiki/Variance
[96] Harmonic Mean - Wikipedia - https://en.wikipedia.org/wiki/Harmonic_mean
[97] Outlier - Wikipedia - https://en.wikipedia.org/wiki/Outlier

```
Harmonic mean: 4.851752022
Arithmetic mean: 8.333333333

Values without outliers
    4   5   3   6   3   5      4   6   6      3

Harmonic mean: 4.166666667
Arithmetic mean: 4.5
```

It is possible to see that using the harmonic mean is an easy way to remove noise in these kinds of datasets.

Crowdsourced testing

A crowdsourced test[98] has been executed, whose CSV records and the **R**[99] script that has been used to parse them, can be seen in the ProfilerExample's crowdtest[100] folder.

Test data have been processed and divided into two big groups, **high-end** and **low-end** devices, by GPU processing power (a device has been marked high-end when its GPU's power was greater than 40 GFLOPS).

Note: you are encouraged to perform the test on your devices and see for yourself the behavior of these test cases.

Test results offer the following observation: NDK implementations get overwhelmed by RenderScript and FilterScript performance almost in any test case.

The following are case-specific observations.

Note: the following charts present a normalized average of results, where, **the smaller the value, the better the performance**.

Memory access

> FilterScript implementations offer the best performance on high-end devices, both in write and read operations.
> Pointers offer good write performance on low-end devices. Also, in this class, there is no clear evidence of a best method for reading from memory.

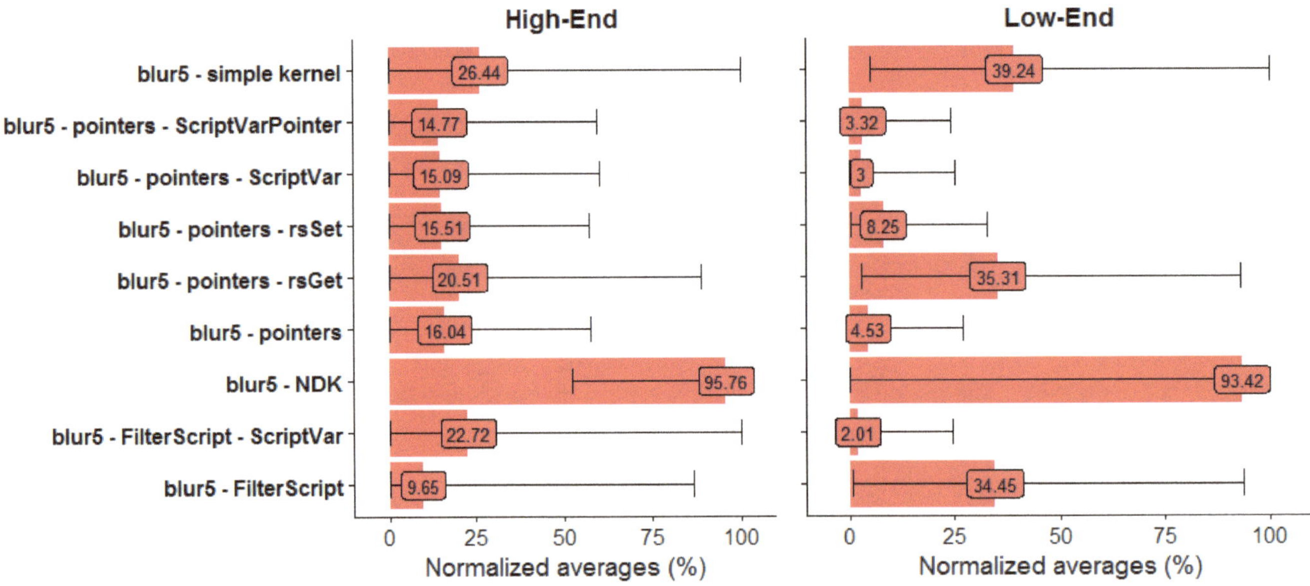

Pure reading performance comparison

---

98 Crowdsourced testing - Wikipedia - https://en.wikipedia.org/wiki/Crowdsourced_testing
99 **R** - https://www.r-project.org/
100 ProfilerExample's crowdtest - https://bitbucket.org/cmaster11/rsbookexamples/src/tip/ProfilerExample/crowdtest

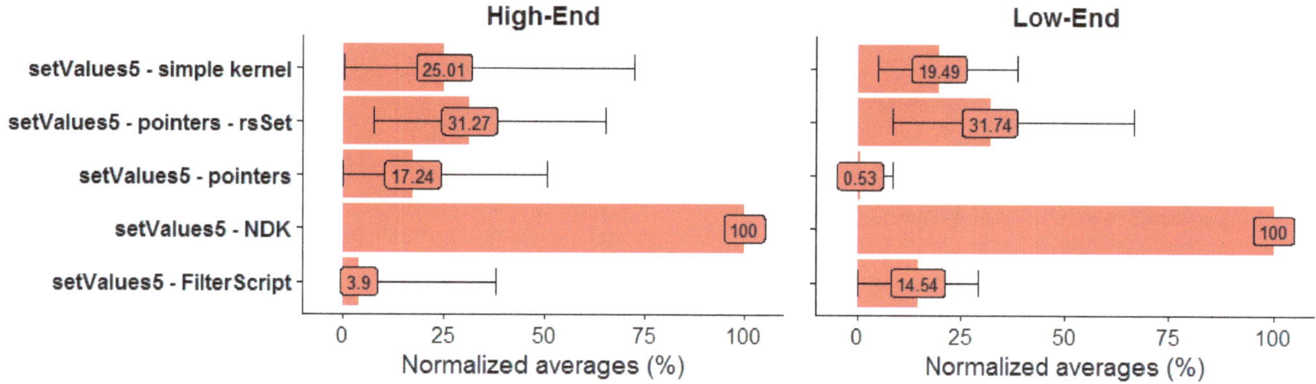

Pure writing performance comparison

Pure calculation

> On high-end devices, FilterScript implementations offer, on average, the best performance for pure calculation. The only countertrending test case is the PI1500 (PI calculation with 1500 iterations per kernel), where simple kernel implementation performs faster than the FilterScript one.

> On low-end devices, FilterScript implementation performs a bit better than the simple kernel one, but not in an overwhelming way.

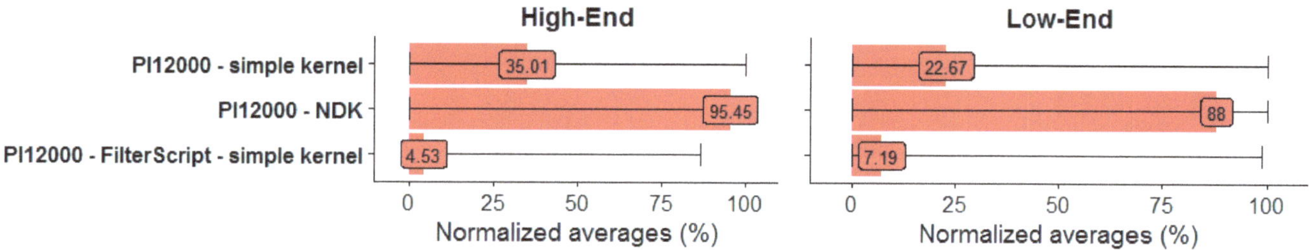

Pure calculation performance comparison

RGBA to grayscale

The grayscale conversion is a process where memory access and pure calculation are similar (both of these operations are very small here, with 1 memory access and three multiplications), and there are no "winners" in the results, neither for the high-end set, nor for the low-end one. Average profiling values (in milliseconds) are too similar (the difference, being in the order of `0.1ms`, makes it impossible to determine the best element, over an average of ~`1.3ms`).

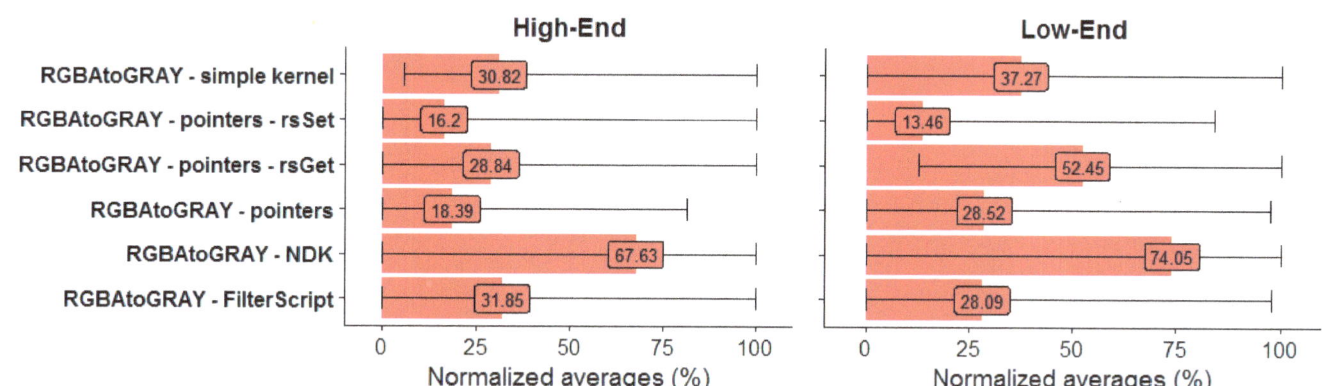

Read and write performance comparison

Kernels calling

Kernels calling methods seem to behave in the same way, because it is not possible to determine a major best method. Average values (in milliseconds) are too similar (the maximum difference is ~1ms on a ~11ms average).

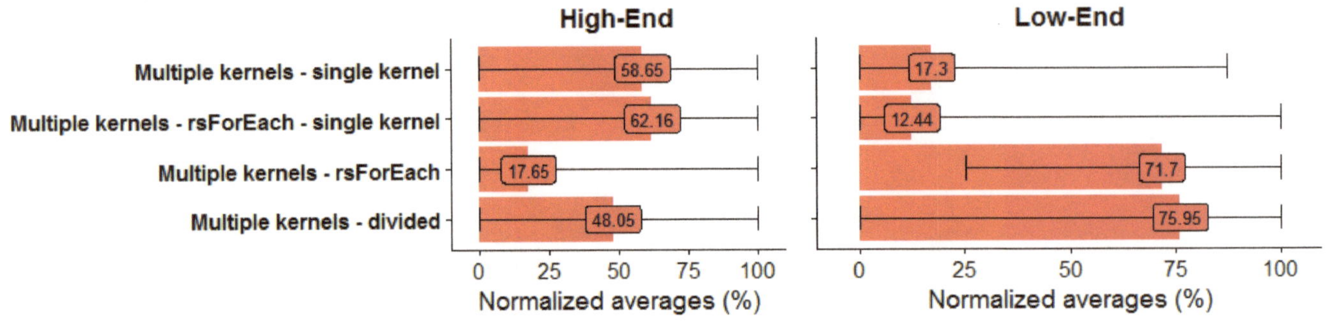

Multiple kernels calling performance

Conclusions

In this chapter I offered an overview about performance in RenderScript, with a crowdsourced test that highlighted how FilterScript is a really good general solution when operating with all kind of devices. To better understand what affects RenderScript performance, the only way is to analyze its internals. The following chapter talks exactly about native RenderScript analysis.

Native analysis

In this chapter I'll describe what's beneath RenderScript, referring directly to Android native (C++) code.

Everything discussed can be found inside the Android source code[101] and, more precisely, by directly cloning RenderScript submodule using the following command:

```
git clone https://android.googlesource.com/platform/frameworks/rs
```

The main topics of this chapter are:

> RenderScript calls workflow: what gets called whenever a common RS function is called.
> RenderScript support library: how to run RS on old devices.
> RenderScript and 64-bit: what changes with this new architecture.
> RenderScript compile and runtime: what builds our RS scripts and what executes them.

Note: To see all RenderScript built-in functions (which can be imported inside every RenderScript script), please refer to Android RenderScript source code[102], or folder `/scriptc`.

RenderScript call workflow

Whenever there is a common (not used to perform computations, like kernels do) RS call, starting from the Java side, a native call is made, pointing out to RenderScript NDK implementation.

Example call stack (Android 23), in case you want to copy an Allocation content to a Bitmap:

Side	Invoked function	File
Java	`Allocation.copyTo(Bitmap)`	`Allocation.java`[103]
Java	`RenderScript. nAllocationCopyToBitmap(...)`	`RenderScript.java`[104]
Java	`RenderScript. rsnAllocationCopyToBitmap(...)`	`RenderScript.java`[105]
C++	`static void nAllocationCopyToBitmap(...)`	`android_renderscript_ RenderScript.cpp`[106] (platform/frameworks/base)
C++	`rsAllocationCopyToBitmap(...)`	`rs.spec`[107]
C++	`void rsi_AllocationCopyToBitmap(...)`	`rsAllocation.cpp`[108]
C++	`void Allocation::read(...)`	`rsAllocation.cpp`[109]

---

[101] Android source code - https://android.googlesource.com
[102] Android RenderScript source code - https://android.googlesource.com/platform/frameworks/rs/+/master/scriptc
[103] Android source code - `renderscript/Allocation.java` - https://android.googlesource.com/platform/frameworks/base/+/marshmallow-mr1-release/rs/java/android/renderscript/Allocation.java#1382
[104] Android source code - `renderscript/RenderScript.java` - https://android.googlesource.com/platform/frameworks/base/+/marshmallow-mr1-release/rs/java/android/renderscript/RenderScript.java#464
[105] Android source code - `renderscript/RenderScript.java` - https://android.googlesource.com/platform/frameworks/base/+/marshmallow-mr1-release/rs/java/android/renderscript/RenderScript.java#463
[106] RenderScript source code - `jni/android_renderscript_RenderScript.cpp` - https://android.googlesource.com/platform/frameworks/base/+/marshmallow-mr1-release/rs/jni/android_renderscript_RenderScript.cpp#1274
[107] RenderScript source code - `rs.spec` - https://android.googlesource.com/platform/frameworks/rs/+/marshmallow-mr1-release/rs.spec#150
[108] RenderScript source code - `rsAllocation.cpp` - https://android.googlesource.com/platform/frameworks/rs/+/marshmallow-mr1-release/rsAllocation.cpp#656

Side	Invoked function	File
C++	`void (*data2D)(...)`	`rs_hal.h`[110]
C++	`void rsdAllocationData2D(...)`	`driver/rsdAllocation.cpp`[111]

What is happening here? Let's see, one by one, what these C++ functions are doing:

`static void nAllocationCopyToBitmap(...)`[112]

This is the interface function between Java and the RS native side. Its purpose is to extract the pointer to input Bitmap's image data and pass it to the next function.

```
static void
nAllocationCopyToBitmap(JNIEnv *_env, jobject _this, jlong con, jlong alloc, jobject jbitmap)
{
    SkBitmap bitmap;
    GraphicsJNI::getSkBitmap(_env, jbitmap, &bitmap);
    bitmap.lockPixels();
    void* ptr = bitmap.getPixels();
    rsAllocationCopyToBitmap((RsContext)con, (RsAllocation)alloc, ptr, bitmap.getSize());
    bitmap.unlockPixels();
    bitmap.notifyPixelsChanged();
}
```

`rsAllocationCopyToBitmap(...)`

This is a binding function, generated during the Android build process, when the `rsg_generator.c`[113] program is called, passing it the `rs.spec`[114] file as input. The functions generated in that program execution are just bridges between the RenderScript JNI side and the RS driver side. They get called even from the RenderScript NDK reflection library. Its `.spec` code is the following:

```
AllocationCopyToBitmap {
    param RsAllocation alloc
    param void * data
}
```

`void rsi_AllocationCopyToBitmap(...)`[115]

This is the entrance function to the RS driver side, a simple bridge to map input Allocation's type and sizes.

```
void rsi_AllocationCopyToBitmap(Context *rsc, RsAllocation va, void *data, size_t sizeBytes) {
    Allocation *a = static_cast<Allocation *>(va);
    const Type * t = a->getType();
```

---

[109] RenderScript source code - `rsAllocation.cpp` - https://android.googlesource.com/platform/frameworks/rs/+/marshmallow-mr1-release/rsAllocation.cpp#228

[110] RenderScript source code - `rs_hal.h` - https://android.googlesource.com/platform/frameworks/rs/+/marshmallow-mr1-release/rs_hal.h#218

[111] RenderScript source code - `driver/rsdAllocation.cpp` - https://android.googlesource.com/platform/frameworks/rs/+/marshmallow-mr1-release/driver/rsdAllocation.cpp#863

[112] RenderScript source code - `jni/android_renderscript_RenderScript.cpp` - https://android.googlesource.com/platform/frameworks/base/+/marshmallow-mr1-release/rs/jni/android_renderscript_RenderScript.cpp#1274

[113] RenderScript source code - `rsg_generator.c` - https://android.googlesource.com/platform/frameworks/rs/+/marshmallow-mr1-release/rsg_generator.c

[114] RenderScript source code - `rs.spec` - https://android.googlesource.com/platform/frameworks/rs/+/marshmallow-mr1-release/rs.spec

[115] RenderScript source code - `rsAllocation.cpp` - https://android.googlesource.com/platform/frameworks/rs/+/marshmallow-mr1-release/rsAllocation.cpp#656

```
    a->read(rsc, 0, 0, 0, RS_ALLOCATION_CUBEMAP_FACE_POSITIVE_X, t->getDimX(), t->getDimY(),
                                                          data, sizeBytes, 0);
}
```

void Allocation::read(...)[116]

This function checks that copy parameters are correct:

> The `stride` variable tells RS the number of bytes occupied by an Allocation's row (in this case we are operating on a 2D matrix, having rows and columns).
> The `sizeBytes` variable contains the total size of elements that have to be copied.

After this check, the RenderScript driver copy function is called.

```
void Allocation::read(Context *rsc, uint32_t xoff, uint32_t yoff,
        uint32_t lod, RsAllocationCubemapFace face, uint32_t w, uint32_t h, void *data,
                                              size_t sizeBytes, size_t stride) {
    const size_t eSize = mHal.state.elementSizeBytes;
    const size_t lineSize = eSize * w;
    if (!stride) {
        stride = lineSize;
    } else {
        if ((lineSize * h) != sizeBytes) {
            char buf[1024];
            sprintf(buf, "Allocation size mismatch, expected %zu, got %zu", (lineSize * h),
                                                          sizeBytes);
            rsc->setError(RS_ERROR_BAD_VALUE, buf);
            return;
        }
    }
    rsc->mHal.funcs.allocation.read2D(rsc, this, xoff, yoff, lod, face, w, h, data,
                                              sizeBytes, stride);
}
```

void (*data2D)(...)[117]

This is a bridge pointer, which points to RenderScript driver implementation. Pointers like this are used, for example, when there is the need to call library functions, knowing only their names and extracting their memory addresses using functions like `dlsym`. For a more precise example, please look at the NativeAllocationMap sample project[118]. This pointer is the *RenderScript driver*'s interface.

RenderScript works by placing calls to its driver. If the driver is not provided by vendors, a standard CPU driver is used. A standard CPU driver source can be found inside the driver[119] RenderScript source folder.

```
void (*data2D)(const Context *rsc, const Allocation *alloc, uint32_t xoff, uint32_t yoff,
                      uint32_t lod, RsAllocationCubemapFace face, uint32_t w, uint32_t h,
                                 const void *data, size_t sizeBytes, size_t stride);
```

Note: from this point, RenderScript functions are shown which belong to the standard CPU RS driver.

---

[116] RenderScript source code - `rsAllocation.cpp` - https://android.googlesource.com/platform/frameworks/rs/+/marshmallow-mr1-release/rsAllocation.cpp#228

[117] RenderScript source code - `rs_hal.h` - https://android.googlesource.com/platform/frameworks/rs/+/marshmallow-mr1-release/rs_hal.h#218

[118] NativeAllocationMap sample project - https://bitbucket.org/cmaster11/rsbookexamples/src/tip/NativeAllocationMap/

[119] RenderScript source code - `driver/` - https://android.googlesource.com/platform/frameworks/rs/+/marshmallow-mr1-release/driver/

void `rsdAllocationData2D(...)`[120]

This is the actual RS CPU driver copy function.

`alloc->mHal.drvState.lod[0].mallocPtr` contains the output Allocation's memory address.

If our output Allocation has a reserved memory block, so `mallocPtr` is not a `nullptr`, then the copy of input data to the output Allocation memory can be done. Otherwise, it means that our output Allocation resides only inside the GPU buffer (it is a texture[121]).

`mHal.state.yuv` is a variable that gets the value passed to the Java function `Type.Builder.setYuvFormat(int)`[122], while creating a new RS Type.

```cpp
void rsdAllocationData2D(const Context *rsc, const Allocation *alloc,
                         uint32_t xoff, uint32_t yoff, uint32_t lod,
                         RsAllocationCubemapFace face, uint32_t w, uint32_t h,
                         const void *data, size_t sizeBytes, size_t stride) {

    DrvAllocation *drv = (DrvAllocation *)alloc->mHal.drv;
    size_t eSize = alloc->mHal.state.elementSizeBytes;
    size_t lineSize = eSize * w;
    if (!stride) {
        stride = lineSize;
    }
    if (alloc->mHal.drvState.lod[0].mallocPtr) {
        const uint8_t *src = static_cast<const uint8_t *>(data);
        uint8_t *dst = GetOffsetPtr(alloc, xoff, yoff, 0, lod, face);
        if (dst == src) {
            // Skip the copy if we are the same allocation. This can arise from our Bitmap
            // optimization, where we share the same storage.
            drv->uploadDeferred = true;
            return;
        }
        for (uint32_t line=yoff; line < (yoff+h); line++) {
            if (alloc->mHal.state.hasReferences) {
                alloc->incRefs(src, w);
                alloc->decRefs(dst, w);
            }
            memcpy(dst, src, lineSize);
            src += stride;
            dst += alloc->mHal.drvState.lod[lod].stride;
        }
        if (alloc->mHal.state.yuv) {
            // Copies YUV aux data
            ...
        }
        drv->uploadDeferred = true;
    } else {
        Update2DTexture(rsc, alloc, data, xoff, yoff, lod, face, w, h);
    }
}
```

---

[120] RenderScript source code - `driver/rsdAllocation.cpp` -
https://android.googlesource.com/platform/frameworks/rs/+/marshmallow-mr1-release/driver/rsdAllocation.cpp#863
[121] Texture - OpenGL Wiki - https://www.opengl.org/wiki/Texture
[122] Android Developers - `Type.Builder.setYuvFormat(int)` -
http://developer.android.com/reference/android/renderscript/Type.Builder.html#setYuvFormat(int)

Bonus function: `static void Update2DTexture(...)`[123]

This function is used by RenderScript to copy a memory block (pointed by `ptr`) over a GPU buffer (whose data is stored inside the `mHal.drv` Allocation member), to store that block as a texture.

```cpp
static void Update2DTexture(const Context *rsc, const Allocation *alloc,
                            const void *ptr, uint32_t xoff, uint32_t yoff, uint32_t lod,
                            RsAllocationCubemapFace face, uint32_t w, uint32_t h) {
#ifndef RS_COMPATIBILITY_LIB
    DrvAllocation *drv = (DrvAllocation *)alloc->mHal.drv;
    rsAssert(drv->textureID);
    RSD_CALL_GL(glBindTexture, drv->glTarget, drv->textureID);
    RSD_CALL_GL(glPixelStorei, GL_UNPACK_ALIGNMENT, 1);
    GLenum t = GL_TEXTURE_2D;
    if (alloc->mHal.state.hasFaces) {
        t = gFaceOrder[face];
    }
    RSD_CALL_GL(glTexSubImage2D, t, lod, xoff, yoff, w, h, drv->glFormat, drv->glType, ptr);
#endif
}
```

The previous workflow is a standard one, which is followed by many RenderScript functions.

RenderScript driver

Pointer functions, like void `(*data2D)(...)`[124], are the interface to access RenderScript driver. The driver is a shared library, loaded at runtime by the RenderScript system, which is the core of RS execution.

The driver is usually provided by the chipset's developers (e.g. Qualcomm provides `libRSDriver_adreno.so` for Adreno GPUs) and is pre-installed on devices. If such a library exists on the device (it may not exist, if there is no dedicated software for the device), it gets loaded using the runtime function `Context::loadDriver`[125]. Otherwise, the `libRSDriver.so` library gets loaded (this is the library built from the `driver`[126] folder, as seen in the main `Android.mk`[127]), providing only plain CPU support (`driver/runtime`[128] folder provides, for example, support for NEON[129] and ASIMD[130] implementations).

Devices containing a custom RS driver can usually rely on GPU support, which becomes extremely relevant for performance matters (FilterScript implementations perform extremely well only in the case of custom RS drivers).

---

[123] RenderScript source code - `driver/rsdAllocation.cpp` - https://android.googlesource.com/platform/frameworks/rs/+/marshmallow-mr1-release/driver/rsdAllocation.cpp#103

[124] RenderScript source code - `rs_hal.h` - https://android.googlesource.com/platform/frameworks/rs/+/marshmallow-mr1-release/rs_hal.h#218

[125] RenderScript source code - `rsDriverLoader.cpp` - https://android.googlesource.com/platform/frameworks/rs/+/marshmallow-mr1-release/rsDriverLoader.cpp#225

[126] RenderScript source code - `driver/` - https://android.googlesource.com/platform/frameworks/rs/+/marshmallow-mr1-release/driver/

[127] RenderScript source code - `Android.mk` - https://android.googlesource.com/platform/frameworks/rs/+/marshmallow-mr1-release/Android.mk#25

[128] RenderScript source code - `driver/runtime/` - https://android.googlesource.com/platform/frameworks/rs/+/marshmallow-mr1-release/driver/runtime/

[129] RenderScript source code - `driver/runtime/arch/neon.ll` - https://android.googlesource.com/platform/frameworks/rs/+/marshmallow-mr1-release/driver/runtime/arch/neon.ll

[130] RenderScript source code - `driver/runtime/arch/asimd.ll` - https://android.googlesource.com/platform/frameworks/rs/+/marshmallow-mr1-release/driver/runtime/arch/asimd.ll

Note: Java pointers

Java's `Allocation` and `RenderScript` classes are simple wrappers of these native ones. Inside Java's Allocation class, you can find a private member, `private long mID`, which contains the actual pointer to the native `Allocation` class, as well as for the `Context` one.

Class	Member name
Allocation	mID
RenderScript	mContext

This could be useful whenever you need to directly access the memory where the Allocation resides, instead of using default RS calls. To have an example of this, please look at the *Native Allocation access* chapter.

RenderScript and 64-bit

With 64-bit devices getting introduced into the market (following the release of Android Lollipop[131], API 21), RenderScript got changed in some ways.

This chapter will refer to Android Marshmallow's RenderScript source code[132].

> It is possible to check if an RS script is being executed on a 64-bit machine by using the following preprocessor directive (inside the `.rs` script):

```
#ifdef __LP64__
// We are in a 64-bit environment
#else
// We are in a 32-bit environment
#endif
```

> Graphics support is deprecated, as can be seen in `api/rs_graphics.spec`[133]:

```
#ifdef __LP64__
// TODO We need to fix some of the builds before enabling this error:
// #error "RenderScript graphics is deprecated and not supported in 64bit mode."
#endif
```

This means no more usage of `rsg` functions, like `rsgAllocationSyncAll`.

A proof of this change can be found at the top of `driver/runtime/rs_mesh.c`[134] or `driver/runtime/rs_program.c`[135], which are not getting compiled on 64-bit machines. Also, all basic graphics structures do not get defined at all, as seen in `rs_hal.h`[136].

---

[131] Android Developers - Android Lollipop - http://developer.android.com/about/versions/lollipop.html
[132] Android Marshmallow's RenderScript source code - https://android.googlesource.com/platform/frameworks/rs/+/marshmallow-mr1-release/
[133] RenderScript source code - `api/rs_graphics.spec` - https://android.googlesource.com/platform/frameworks/rs/+/marshmallow-mr1-release/api/rs_graphics.spec#22
[134] `driver/runtime/rs_mesh.c` - https://android.googlesource.com/platform/frameworks/rs/+/marshmallow-mr1-release/driver/runtime/rs_mesh.c
[135] `driver/runtime/rs_program.c` - https://android.googlesource.com/platform/frameworks/rs/+/marshmallow-mr1-release/driver/runtime/rs_program.c
[136] `rs_hal.h` - https://android.googlesource.com/platform/frameworks/rs/+/marshmallow-mr1-release/rs_hal.h#102

> Internal reference to basic RS objects (like Allocations) is made with new elements, as can be seen in `api/rs_object_types.spec`[137]:

```
#ifndef __LP64__
    #define _RS_HANDLE \
    struct {\
        const int* const p;\
    } __attribute__((packed, aligned(4)))
#else
    #define _RS_HANDLE \
    struct {\
        const long* const p;\
        const long* const r;\
        const long* const v1;\
        const long* const v2;\
    }
#endif
```

These fields gets filled, for example when instantiating an allocation, with the following elements:

```
// Pointer to the memory allocation
obj->r = alloc->mHal.drvState.lod[0].mallocPtr;
obj->v1 = alloc->mHal.drv;
obj->v2 = (void *)alloc->mHal.drvState.lod[0].stride;
```

> When invoking a script using `rsForEach` function, as can be seen in the *rsForEach paragraph*, it is not necessary to pass custom user data size anymore. This can be seen in `driver/rsdRuntimeStubs.cpp`[138]:

```
// These functions are only supported in 32-bit.
#ifndef __LP64__
void __attribute__((overloadable)) rsForEach(::rs_script script, ::rs_allocation in,
                                ::rs_allocation out, const void *usr, uint32_t usrLen) {
    Context *rsc = RsdCpuReference::getTlsContext();
    rsrForEach(rsc, (Script *)script.p, (Allocation *)in.p, (Allocation *)out.p, usr,
                                                            usrLen, nullptr);
}
void __attribute__((overloadable)) rsForEach(::rs_script script, ::rs_allocation in,
                                ::rs_allocation out, const void *usr,
                                uint32_t usrLen, const rs_script_call *call) {
    Context *rsc = RsdCpuReference::getTlsContext();
    rsrForEach(rsc, (Script *)script.p, (Allocation *)in.p, (Allocation *)out.p, usr,
                                                            usrLen, (RsScriptCall *)call);
}
#endif
```

---

[137] RenderScript source code - `api/rs_object_types.spec` -
https://android.googlesource.com/platform/frameworks/rs/+/marshmallow-mr1-release/api/rs_object_types.spec#26
[138] RenderScript source code - `driver/rsdRuntimeStubs.cpp` -
https://android.googlesource.com/platform/frameworks/rs/+/marshmallow-mr1-release/driver/rsdRuntimeStubs.cpp#464

> Careful attention must be paid if accessing Allocations directly using pointers, like how it happens in the *Native Allocation access chapter*, because 64-bit pointers occupy more memory than 32-bit ones. A proof of this can be seen in the `driver/runtime/rs_structs.h`[139] file, where padding caused by parent class (`ObjectBase`[140]) is incremented because of pointers size:

```
typedef struct Allocation {
#ifndef __LP64__
    char __pad[32];
#else
    char __pad[56];
#endif
```

Note: a discussion over this padding can be found inside the *mallocPtr member* section.

RenderScript compile and runtime

RenderScript compile/usage workflow is as follows:

> The *slang* compiler is used by Android SDK at compile-time, where optimizations are made to RS scripts, which then gets translated to bitcode (`.bc`) files.
> *libbcc* is called upon RS code execution. As stated in its README[141], this library's implementation can be customized by vendors, having it optimized per-device.

slang - Compiler for RenderScript language

The RenderScript code is compiled using `llvm-rs-cc` (codename: `slang`), an LLVM[142] Google variant. You can find its source cloning its repository:

`git clone https://android.googlesource.com/platform/frameworks/compile/slang`

Its main tasks are:

> Compiling C99-like code into bitcode files (.bc), which get loaded at runtime.
> Generating Java source files that map RenderScript components (to invoke RS elements from the Java side). Reference: slang_rs_reflection.cpp[143].
> Generating C++ source files when building RenderScript scripts in *NDK native mode*. Reference: slang_rs_reflection_cpp.cpp[144].

Note: I suggest you read its `README.rst`[145] file, which can help understanding the whole argument.

Note: inside the file slang_rs_export_type.cpp[146] it is possible to find a list of all RS predefined types (variable gReflectionTypes[]).

---

[139] RenderScript source code - `driver/runtime/rs_structs.h` - https://android.googlesource.com/platform/frameworks/rs/+/marshmallow-mr1-release/driver/runtime/rs_structs.h#31
[140] RenderScript source code - `rsObjectBase.cpp` - https://android.googlesource.com/platform/frameworks/rs/+/marshmallow-mr1-release/rsObjectBase.cpp
[141] libbcc source code - README - https://android.googlesource.com/platform/frameworks/compile/libbcc/+/marshmallow-release/README.rst
[142] LLVM - http://llvm.org/
[143] RenderScript source code - `slang_rs_reflection.cpp` - https://android.googlesource.com/platform/frameworks/compile/slang/+/marshmallow-mr1-release/slang_rs_reflection.cpp
[144] RenderScript source code - `slang_rs_reflection_cpp.cpp` - https://android.googlesource.com/platform/frameworks/compile/slang/+/marshmallow-mr1-release/slang_rs_reflection_cpp.cpp
[145] slang source code - `README.rst` - https://android.googlesource.com/platform/frameworks/compile/slang/+/marshmallow-release/README.rst
[146] RenderScript source code - slang_rs_export_type.cpp - https://android.googlesource.com/platform/frameworks/compile/slang/+/marshmallow-mr1-release/slang_rs_export_type.cpp#49

libbcc - Executor of RenderScript bitcode resources

RenderScript compiled bitcode (.bc) files are handled at runtime by **libbcc**, an Android module that you can find by cloning its repository:

```
git clone https://android.googlesource.com/platform/frameworks/compile/libbcc
```

Its main task is to load bitcode files, linking them with device-specific provided RenderScript drivers. It also stores linked files using a caching system, which lets application launch faster on following executions.

For a detailed explanation, please refer to libbcc's README[147].

Diagram

A general diagram follows, which explains how the entire process works:

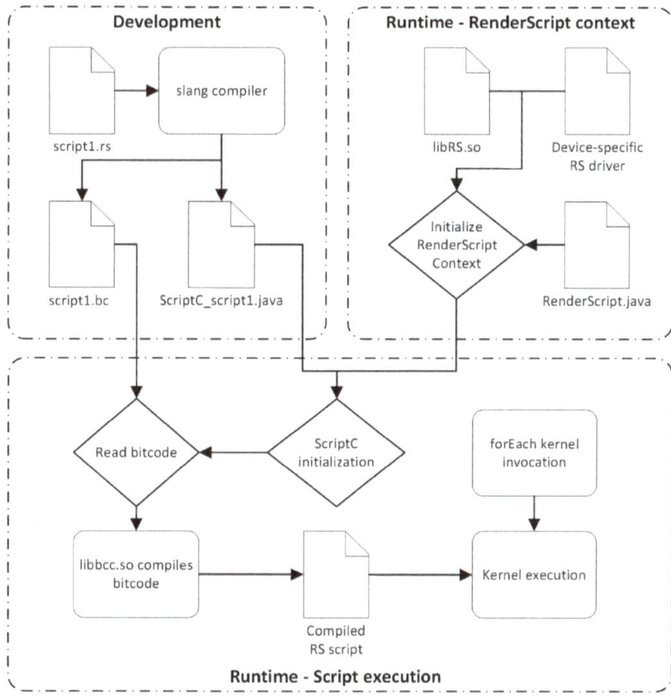

RenderScript runtime execution diagram

Conclusions

In this chapter I gave an overview of how RenderScript behaves underneath the surface, starting from the fact that every Java call triggers a C++ library JNI call, which then triggers a RenderScript driver process. Knowing how RS works, on the C++ side, makes it possible to take advantage of this behavior, to perform non-common (at least not publicly documented) actions, like accessing Allocations contents directly, using pointers and standard C++ code. Some of these actions are covered in the next chapter.

---

[147] libbcc's README - https://android.googlesource.com/platform/frameworks/compile/libbcc/+/marshmallow-mr1-release/README.rst

RenderScript and NDK

It is possible to access RenderScript elements from the NDK side of Android. Below are presented some hacky ways to achieve this goal, using both Java reflection[148] and direct RenderScript shared library function mapping.

> Accessing RenderScript elements using Java reflection and direct pointer access.
> Using RenderScript native NDK C++ side support to perform operations.

NOTICE: the following sections demonstrate experimental methods, which could be not consistent among different devices (having then different RenderScript drivers). You are encouraged, however, to test them, because exploring RenderScript inner mechanics is a huge help in understanding how it works.

Access RenderScript elements using Java reflection

This process works with a simple workflow:

1. Retrieve an Allocation/Kernel C++ pointer using Java reflection.
2. Use this pointer from the NDK side to perform actions.

Allocation pointer access

You can find an example of the following process inside the NativeAllocationMap sample project[149].

To get the right memory address, there are few steps to follow:

> Getting the allocation `mID` private element, which contains the native pointer to the C++ `android::renderscript::Allocation`[150] class.
> Getting the `mHal.drvState.lod[0].mallocPtr` member contents.
> Retrieving the allocation contents.

Note: It is necessary to call the `mRS.finish()` function before accessing the Allocation natively, because kernels are not synchronous to Java but only to their RS context. Finish function waits for all kernels to complete their calculations (for a discussion on this, refer to *RenderScript components* chapter's *Kernel* section).

Get Allocation mID

The `Allocation` Java class contains a private member (inherited from the `BaseObj` one) called `mID`. Upon instantiating the Allocation, this member gets filled with the pointer to the C++ `android::renderscript::Allocation`[151] class. Using this pointer, then, makes it possible to access many C++ side RenderScript elements.

Create this function inside your app code:

```java
long getAllocationPointer(Allocation allocation) {
    Field allocationIDField = null;
    long AllocationID = 0;
    try {
        allocationIDField = allocation.getClass().getSuperclass().getDeclaredField("mID");
        allocationIDField.setAccessible(true);
        AllocationID = (long) allocationIDField.getLong(allocation);
    } catch (IllegalAccessException e) {
        throw new RuntimeException("Could not access Allocation ID");
```

---

[148] Java - Reflection - https://docs.oracle.com/javase/tutorial/reflect/

[149] NativeAllocationMap sample project - https://bitbucket.org/cmaster11/rsbookexamples/src/tip/NativeAllocationMap/

[150] RenderScript source code - `rsAllocation.h` - https://android.googlesource.com/platform/frameworks/rs/+/marshmallow-mr1-release/rsAllocation.h

[151] RenderScript source code - `rsAllocation.h` - https://android.googlesource.com/platform/frameworks/rs/+/marshmallow-mr1-release/rsAllocation.h

```java
    } catch (NoSuchFieldException e) {
        throw new RuntimeException("Could not find Allocation ID");
    }

    if (AllocationID == 0) {
        throw new RuntimeException("Invalid allocation ID");
    }
    return AllocationID;
}
```

Calling it, passing your Allocation element, will retrieve the actual address of the native Allocation class. This function simply accesses the `mID` private member and reads its value using reflection.

`mallocPtr` member

Note: If you don't know how to enable the NDK support please look at the *Enable NDK support* appendix to do this.

Among the members of the `android::renderscript::Allocation` class, the `mHal.drvState.lod[0].mallocPtr` one is defined: this is a pointer that directly points the Allocation memory block.

Depending upon the target Android API version, there are two possible ways to get the pointer address:

> For API levels < 21, direct memory offset calculation must be used.
> For API levels >= 21, the `Allocation::getPointer`[152] function is available.

API level < 21

To get the value of this pointer, you need to know its location inside the memory. To calculate this location, you need to calculate the address offset generated by `Allocation` class members.

Note: an important notice is that the code written using the NDK direct pointer access uses the RenderScript library installed on the phone. This means that, if the device has Android 19, it will require a different mapping than a device having Android 18.

This process can be easily accomplished analyzing the `rsAllocation.h`[153] Android source file, for every wanted API version. The Allocation class source code begins with:

```cpp
class Allocation : public ObjectBase {
    public:
        const static int MAX_LOD = 16;
        struct Hal {
            void * drv;
            struct State {
                const Type * type;
                ...
                void *deprecated02;
            };
            State state;
            struct DrvState {
                struct LodState {
                    void * mallocPtr;
                    ...
```

Note: a good read about this topic is **The Lost Art of C Structure Packing**[154].

---

[152] RenderScript source code - `rsAllocation.cpp` - https://android.googlesource.com/platform/frameworks/rs/+/marshmallow-mr1-release/rsAllocation.cpp#160
[153] RenderScript source code - `rsAllocation.h` - https://android.googlesource.com/platform/frameworks/rs/+/jb-mr2-release/rsAllocation.h
[154] Eric S. Raymond - The Lost Art of C Structure Packing - http://www.catb.org/esr/structure-packing/

The offset calculation process involves two steps:

> Calculating the offset provided by `ObjectBase`[155] class, which the `Allocation` one extends.
> Calculating the offset generated by the `Allocation`[156] class members.

The following example applies to API 18, but can be applied to all other versions.

Note: Android API versions lower than 21 provide no 64-bit support, so calculations will be done here only for 32-bit architectures.

ObjectBase: to calculate the padding generated by the `ObjectBase` class, it is necessary to analyze contained variables and calculate their size.

> At least one `virtual` function exists, so the elements list begins with 1 pointer.
> `String8`[157] is a utility class which contains only a pointer.
> Remove from the list all `static` variables and all methods.

The remaining elements are:

Element	Size
`Context *mRSC;`	1 pointer
`String8 mName;`	1 pointer
`mutable int32_t mSysRefCount;`	4 bytes
`mutable int32_t mUserRefCount;`	4 bytes
`mutable const ObjectBase * mPrev;`	1 pointer
`mutable const ObjectBase * mNext;`	1 pointer
`DebugHelper *mDH;`	1 pointer

The final list is made of 6 pointers and 8 bytes.

The calculated size is 32 bytes, because in 32-bit systems a pointer occupies 4 bytes.

Allocation: the same process, which has been applied to the `ObjectBase` class, applies to the `Allocation` class.

1. Virtual functions exist, but they don't need to be taken into account because the vtable[158] pointer has already been declared by the `ObjectBase` class.
2. Remove from the list all `static` variables and all methods.

The remaining elements are, to reach the `mallocPtr` variable:

Element	Size (bytes)
Previously calculated `ObjectBase`	32
`struct Hal {`	...
`void * drv;`	4
`struct State {`	...
`const Type * type;`	4
`uint32_t usageFlags;`	4

---

[155] RenderScript source code - `rsObjectBase.h` - https://android.googlesource.com/platform/frameworks/rs/+/jb-mr2-release/rsObjectBase.h
[156] RenderScript source code - `rsAllocation.h` - https://android.googlesource.com/platform/frameworks/rs/+/jb-mr2-release/rsAllocation.h
[157] Android source code - `include/utils/String8.h` - https://android.googlesource.com/platform/frameworks/native/+/jb-mr2-release/include/utils/String8.h
[158] Virtual method table - Wikipedia - https://en.wikipedia.org/wiki/Virtual_method_table

Element	Size (bytes)
`RsAllocationMipmapControl mipmapControl;`	4
`uint32_t yuv;`	4
`uint32_t elementSizeBytes;`	4
`bool hasMipmaps;`	1
`bool hasFaces;`	1
`bool hasReferences;`	1
Padding to get alignment for `void *`	1
`void * userProvidedPtr;`	4
`int32_t surfaceTextureID;`	4
`void *deprecated01;`	4
`void *deprecated02;`	4
...	...
`void * mallocPtr;`	...
Total	**76**

A pointer occupies 4 bytes, total `struct State` size is 40 bytes. Aux padding is not needed because 40 is already a multiple of 4 (which is the largest element size in the `struct`).

Calculated final offset is:

`sizeof(ObjectBase) + sizeof(void *) + sizeof(struct State) = 32 bytes + 4 bytes + 40 bytes = 76 bytes`

Once the final offset is known, it can be used to get the `mallocPtr` member:

```c
// Pass your native side the Allocation's mID (AllocationID)
JNIEXPORT void JNICALL
Java_..._MainActivity_executeNativeExtraction(JNIEnv *env, jobject, jlong AllocationID)
{
    // Casts pointer address void *
    void *pointerAddress = (void *) AllocationID;

    // E.g. API 18
    size_t offset = 76;

    // Retrieves memory pointer
    void *mallocPtr = *(void **) (pointerAddress + offset);

    // Do your operations, e.g. extract the Allocation data...

    // Example of copying some data
    int values[10];
    // memcpy(destination, source, bytes size)
    memcpy(&values, mallocPtr, 3 * sizeof(int));
}
```

API level >= 21

From API 21 onwards, the C++ Allocation::getPointer[159] function is available, and can be used invoking the rsAllocationGetPointer[160] function (please look at the *Native kernel calling* section to understand how to do it), declared as follows (rsAllocation.cpp[161]):

```cpp
void *rsi_AllocationGetPointer(Context *rsc, RsAllocation valloc,
                                    uint32_t lod, RsAllocationCubemapFace face, uint32_t z,
                                    uint32_t array, size_t *stride, size_t strideLen) {
    Allocation *alloc = static_cast<Allocation *>(valloc);
    rsAssert(strideLen == sizeof(size_t));

    return alloc->getPointer(rsc, lod, face, z, array, stride);
}
```

A sample invocation of this function, as seen in the NativeAllocationMap sample project[162], is as follows:

```cpp
// void *rsi_AllocationGetPointer(Context *rsc, RsAllocation valloc,
//      uint32_t lod, RsAllocationCubemapFace face,
//      uint32_t z, uint32_t array, size_t *stride, size_t strideLen)
mallocPtr = fnPointers->AllocationGetPointer(contextPtr, allocationPtr, 0, 0, 0, 0, 0,sizeof(size_t));
```

The root function, in this case, is as follows:

```cpp
void * Allocation::getPointer(const Context *rsc, uint32_t lod, RsAllocationCubemapFace face,
                                    uint32_t z, uint32_t array, size_t *stride) {

    if ( (lod >= mHal.drvState.lodCount) ||
        (z && (z >= mHal.drvState.lod[lod].dimZ)) ||
        ((face != RS_ALLOCATION_CUBEMAP_FACE_POSITIVE_X) && !mHal.state.hasFaces) ||
        (array != 0) ) {
        return nullptr;
    }

    if (mRSC->mHal.funcs.allocation.getPointer != nullptr) {
        // Notify the driver, if present that the user is mapping the buffer
        mRSC->mHal.funcs.allocation.getPointer(rsc, this, lod, face, z, array);
    }

    size_t s = 0;
    if ((stride != nullptr) && mHal.drvState.lod[0].dimY) {
        *stride = mHal.drvState.lod[lod].stride;
    }
    return mHal.drvState.lod[lod].mallocPtr;
}
```

Note: if you are using RenderScript with its *NDK native support*, this function can be directly accessed using the android::RSC::Allocation::getPointer[163] one. Be aware that, in this case, the Allocation must be initialized with the RS_ALLOCATION_USAGE_SHARED flag.

---

[159] RenderScript source code - `rsAllocation.cpp` - https://android.googlesource.com/platform/frameworks/rs/+/marshmallow-mr1-release/rsAllocation.cpp#160

[160] RenderScript source code - `rs.spec` - https://android.googlesource.com/platform/frameworks/rs/+/marshmallow-mr1-release/rs.spec#155

[161] RenderScript source code - `rsAllocation.cpp` - https://android.googlesource.com/platform/frameworks/rs/+/marshmallow-mr1-release/rsAllocation.cpp#844

[162] NativeAllocationMap sample project - https://bitbucket.org/cmaster11/rsbookexamples/src/tip/NativeAllocationMap/

[163] RenderScript source code - `cpp/Allocation.cpp` - https://android.googlesource.com/platform/frameworks/rs/+/marshmallow-mr1-release/cpp/Allocation.cpp#169

Native kernel calling

It is possible to directly call a kernel function of an RS script from the NDK side, using its native NDK support, as discussed *below*.

I want to offer a different approach, mostly because operating only with Java is usually easier (considering the "code writing and debugging" side). What will be required is only to access an RS library function that will trigger our scripts kernels.

As can be seen in the `cpp/Script.cpp`[164] file, the following function is called to execute a kernel:

```
RS::dispatch->ScriptForEach(mRS->getContext(), getID(), slot, in_id, out_id, usr, usrLen, nullptr, 0);
```

The `ScriptForEach` function pointer is defined inside `cpp/rsDispatch.h`[165], and its address is loaded in the `cpp/rsDispatch.cpp`[166] source file:

```
dispatchTab.ScriptForEach = (ScriptForEachFnPtr)dlsym(handle, "rsScriptForEach");
```

The definition of this function is built together with the Android SDK build process, and its existence can be proved inspecting the `libRS.so` library file (that comes together with and Android phone, inside `/system/lib` directory) using a tool like `readelf`[167], that will output the following entry (under the `.dynsym` table), or a similar one:

```
1087: 0002afe9    216 FUNC    GLOBAL DEFAULT    9 rsScriptForEach
```

This means that actually, loading the `libRS.so` library in a dynamic way, you can call this function as you will know its memory address.

The process required to obtain its memory address can be explained by the following C++ code:

```cpp
#include <dlfcn.h>

// Handle to libRS.so library
void *libRShandle;

// Declaration of RS forEach function pointer. Required args can be seen
// in its definition inside rsScript.cpp file:
//
// void rsi_ScriptForEach(Context *rsc, RsScript vs, uint32_t slot,
//                                      RsAllocation vain, RsAllocation vaout,
//                                      const void *params, size_t paramLen,
//                                      const RsScriptCall *sc, size_t scLen)
//
// Reference:
// https://android.googlesource.com/platform/frameworks/rs/+/marshmallow-mr1-release/rsScript.cpp#210
//
// Types reference:
// https://android.googlesource.com/platform/frameworks/rs/+/marshmallow-mr1-release/rsDefines.h#43
//
// * rsc is the pointer to a RS context
// * vs is the pointer to a RS script
// * slot is the integer representing the kernel index that has to be called.
// * vain and vaout are pointers to input and output allocations
// * params is custom user data struct pointer.
```

---

[164] RenderScript source code - `cpp/Script.cpp` - https://android.googlesource.com/platform/frameworks/rs/+/marshmallow-mr1-release/cpp/Script.cpp#36

[165] RenderScript source code - `cpp/rsDispatch.h` - https://android.googlesource.com/platform/frameworks/rs/+/marshmallow-mr1-release/cpp/rsDispatch.h#161

[166] RenderScript source code - `cpp/rsDispatch.cpp` - https://android.googlesource.com/platform/frameworks/rs/+/marshmallow-mr1-release/cpp/rsDispatch.cpp#263

[167] readelf tool - https://sourceware.org/binutils/docs/binutils/readelf.html

```c
// * paramLen is user data struct size.
// * sc is a LaunchOptions pointer, which restrains the kernel
//      usage, for example limiting initial X or Y.
// * scLen is the actual size of the LaunchOptions struct.
int (*rsScriptForEach)(void *, void *, int, void *, void *, void *, int, void *, int);


void loadLibRS() {

    // Loads libRS.so headers to find function address.
    // More info can be found here: http://linux.die.net/man/3/dlopen
    libRShandle = dlopen("libRS.so", RTLD_LOCAL | RTLD_LAZY);

    // Loads functions into our variable
    *(void **) (&rsScriptForEach) = dlsym(libRShandle, "rsScriptForEach");
}
```

Once you have the `rsScriptForEach` function's pointer, you can call it and pass our arguments (example taken directly from our NativeAllocationMap sample project[168]:

```c
JNIEXPORT bool JNICALL
Java_net_hydex11_..._executeNativeKernel(JNIEnv *env, jobject, jlong ContextID,
                           jlong ScriptID, jlong AllocationInID, jlong AllocationOutID) {

    // Struct that contains references to the RS lib functions
    RSFnPointers * fnPointers;

    // Load the RS lib functions
    if((fnPointers = loadLibRSForNativeKernel()) == NULL)
        return false;

    // Invoke forEach for our kernel "sum2", which has slot 2,
    // because it is the second, non "root" named, declared function.
    int kernelSlot = 2;

    ...

    fnPointers->ScriptForEach((void *) ContextID, (void *) ScriptID, kernelSlot,
                         (void *) AllocationInID, (void *) AllocationOutID, 0, 0, 0, 0);
    ...
}
```

The previous code will execute the chosen kernel over input and output allocations. The benefits of this process are (for example):

> You can manage initialization using only the Java side (like instantiating the RS Context, Elements and Allocations).
> In case you are doing heavy computing operations in the NDK, you can store elements inside the input Allocation directly using its memory pointer (as seen before) and execute a kernel over it without the need to ask the Java side to do it (this would slow down everything in real-time operations). Then, retrieving the result from output Allocation memory pointer would be an immediate process.
> In case you are using an external library (which you connect to with your NDK but this is not directly integrated into your Android project) you can just set it up to receive the pointers to Allocations and kernel calling functions, to trigger heavy computations without the need to bind the library to your own environment.

---

[168] NativeAllocationMap sample project - https://bitbucket.org/cmaster11/rsbookexamples/src/tip/NativeAllocationMap/

RenderScript NDK native support

Google made a native binding available for our RS scripts, so that technically you can use automatically generated code (built exactly as it happens when using Java) from the NDK side, using .h includes. You can see a sample of this process in Google's HelloComputeNDK example[169].

The RSNDKExample sample project[170] shows the steps required to run the sample RS code on the NDK side.

Setup

What is required to enable this native support mode is to:

> Set up the NDK as described in the *External ndk-build implementation* chapter.
> Create the RenderScript folder (as shown in the *Setup RenderScript* topic).
> Set the following gradle setting:

```
// Min API that supports RS C++ side is 19
minSdkVersion 19
```

> Set the Android.mk file to match the following contents. Specific settings are required to enable RenderScript support, and binding the RScpp_static library is a required step:

```
LOCAL_PATH := $(call my-dir)
include $(CLEAR_VARS)

# Module name, produces libRSNDK.so
LOCAL_MODULE := RSNDK
LOCAL_LDLIBS += -llog -landroid -lc -lz -lm

### RS setup
# Include all RS C++ headers and generated sources
LOCAL_C_INCLUDES += $(TARGET_C_INCLUDES)/rs/cpp \
    $(TARGET_C_INCLUDES)/rs

# Links required RS library
LOCAL_LDFLAGS += -L$(call host-path,$(TARGET_C_INCLUDES)/../lib/rs)
LOCAL_LDLIBS += -lRScpp_static

# Automatically includes all .rs and .fs files that reside in the
# app/src/main/rs folder
# Reference: http://stackoverflow.com/a/8980441/3671330
RS_FOLDER := $(LOCAL_PATH)/../rs
RS_SRC_FILES := $(wildcard $(RS_FOLDER)/*.rs)
RS_SRC_FILES += $(wildcard $(RS_FOLDER)/*.fs)

# Here, __ folder is included. It contains RS generated headers.
# It is named this way because dots were replaced by underscores.
# ../rs/main.rs -> __/rs/ScriptC_main.h
LOCAL_C_INCLUDES += $(TARGET_OBJS)/$(LOCAL_MODULE)/__

# FYI:
# TARGET_OBJS folder can be:
#   app/build/intermediates/ndk/obj/local/armeabi-v7a/objs
# LOCAL_MODULE is: RSNDK

# Removes first part of path to make it acceptable
```

---

[169] HelloComputeNDK example - https://android.googlesource.com/platform/frameworks/rs/+/marshmallow-release/java/tests/HelloComputeNDK/
[170] RSNDKExample sample project - https://bitbucket.org/cmaster11/rsbookexamples/src/tip/RSNDKExample/

```
# by LOCAL_SRC_FILES
RS_SRC_FILES := $(RS_SRC_FILES:$(LOCAL_PATH)/%=%)

# C++ sources
LOCAL_SRC_FILES := main.cpp $(RS_SRC_FILES)

include $(BUILD_SHARED_LIBRARY)
```

> Set the `Application.mk` file to match the following content. The `stlport_static` library is suggested to run the RS code, as well as android-19 is the minimum Android API version that supports the RS C++ side.

```
APP_STL := stlport_static
APP_ABI := armeabi-v7a # Add other platforms here
APP_PLATFORM := android-19
```

> Inside your C++ code, include RenderScript header files:

>> Include all RenderScript default headers: `#include <RenderScript.h>`.
>> Include RenderScript generated headers, following .rs files' relative paths (e.g. `rs/main.rs ->` `rs/ScriptC_main.h`): `#include "rs/ScriptC_main.h"`.

C++ code

All C++ code references can be found inside the Android RS source's `cpp`[171] folder. The RS classes, structs, etc, can be found inside the `cpp/rsCppStructs.h`[172] source file. RS defines, like enum, can be found inside the `rsDefines.h`[173] source file.

Namespace

All code shown here uses the `android::RSC` namespace. It can be automatically included using this code:

```
using namespace android::RSC;
```

Initialize RS context

To initialize a RenderScript context, the following code can be used:

```
// Define a pointer to a RS context
sp <RS> mRS;

void initRS(const char *cacheDir, bool useDebugMode){
    // Instantiates the RS context
    mRS = new RS();

    // Initialize the RS context
    mRS->init(cacheDir, useDebugMode ? RS_CONTEXT_TYPE_DEBUG : RS_CONTEXT_TYPE_NORMAL);
}
```

Note: The `RS_CONTEXT_TYPE_DEBUG` constant represents the same concept as the one shown in the *RS context's debug note* topic.

Note: `sp<RS>` is a StrongPointer[174].

---

[171] RenderScript source code - `cpp/` - https://android.googlesource.com/platform/frameworks/rs/+/marshmallow-mr1-release/cpp/
[172] RenderScript source code - `cpp/rsCppStructs.h` - https://android.googlesource.com/platform/frameworks/rs/+/marshmallow-mr1-release/cpp/rsCppStructs.h
[173] RenderScript source code - `rsDefines.h` - https://android.googlesource.com/platform/frameworks/rs/+/marshmallow-mr1-release/rsDefines.h
[174] RenderScript source code - `cpp/util/StrongPointer.h` - https://android.googlesource.com/platform/frameworks/rs/+/marshmallow-mr1-release/cpp/util/StrongPointer.h#63

To call this function from the Java side, a JNI binding is needed:

```cpp
// Bound to net.hydex11.rsndkexample.MainActivity class.
//
// Java side:
// static native void
//       initRenderScript(String cacheDir, boolean useDebugMode);

JNIEXPORT void
Java_net_hydex11_rsndkexample_MainActivity_initRenderScript(JNIEnv* env, jobject jObj,
                                                jstring cacheDirObj, jboolean useDebugMode){

    // Retrieves bytes from Java side to NDK one
    const char *cacheDir = env->GetStringUTFChars(cacheDirObj, NULL);

    // Initialize RS context
    initRS(cacheDir, useDebugMode);

    env->ReleaseStringUTFChars(cacheDirObj, cacheDir);
}
```

The cacheDirObj variable is a string containing the path to the app's cache directory. Its value can be obtained from the Java side, using the getCacheDir() function:

```java
String cacheDirPath = getCacheDir().getAbsolutePath();
initRenderScript(cacheDirPath, BuildConfig.DEBUG);
```

The example

The RSNDKExample sample project[175] shows how to run a simple multiplying kernel over an RS allocation.

> Input is a series of numbers, like 0, 1, 2, ..., 14, 15.
> Output is a series made by multiplying input by 10, using the following kernel function:

```cpp
void mulKernel(const int *v_in, int *v_out){
    *v_out = *v_in * 10;
}
```

The sample project's main function, runNDKExample(), is as follows:

```cpp
void runNDKExample() {

    LOGD("Running NDK example");

    const int inputElementsCount = 16;

    int inputArray[inputElementsCount];

    // Fills the input data with some values
    for (int i = 0; i < inputElementsCount; i++) {
        inputArray[i] = i;
    }
    // inputArray will now range from 0 to 15

    LOGD("Filled sample input data");

    // Instantiates an Allocation and copies the sample data inside it
    sp <Allocation> inputAllocationSimple = Allocation::createSized(mRS, Element::I32(mRS),
                                                inputElementsCount);
```

---

[175] RSNDKExample sample project - https://bitbucket.org/cmaster11/rsbookexamples/src/tip/RSNDKExample/

```cpp
inputAllocationSimple->copy1DFrom((void *) inputArray);

// Debugs allocation contents
debugAllocationSimpleCopy("inputAllocationSimple", inputAllocationSimple);

// Output allocation where to store results
sp <Allocation> outputAllocation = Allocation::createSized(mRS, Element::I32(mRS),
                                                           inputElementsCount);

// Init custom script
ScriptC_main *myScript = new ScriptC_main(mRS);

// Execute kernel on simple allocation and debug it
myScript->forEach_mulKernel(inputAllocationSimple, outputAllocation);
mRS->finish();

// outputAllocation will now contain input elements, multiplied by 10
debugAllocationSimpleCopy("inputAllocationSimple -> outputAllocation", outputAllocation);
}
```

Notes

One problem of this mode is the missing support of custom struct elements, as I discussed in the *RenderScript components* chapter.

Custom structs are not yet supported (Android 23). All you get while building a project is:

```
RSExportType::ExportClassRecord not implemented
```

To see what is supported, please look at the slang compiler in the Android source code[176].

Another problem is that, in the Android NDK, release r11, it is not possible to use RenderScript C++ implementation. Library and headers are not available[177]. The latest (as of May, 2016) NDK version with native RenderScript C++ support is the r10e one.

Conclusions

This chapter has shown how to use the NDK side to directly access RenderScript memory allocations and how to directly invoke its C++ library functions. Now comes the time to explore different use cases, to demonstrate RenderScript power. The next chapter will show these.

---

[176] slang source code - `slang_rs_export_type.cpp` -
https://android.googlesource.com/platform/frameworks/compile/slang/+/marshmallow-release/slang_rs_export_type.cpp#1594
[177] NDK issues: no renderscript headers/library in r11 - GitHub - https://github.com/android-ndk/ndk/issues/7

Use cases

The following are some use cases and examples of common functions. Also, some use cases provide real example projects to test them.

Debug

If you need to debug RenderScript scripts, you can use the `rsDebug` function:

```
rsDebug("Here is some text!", value1, value2, value3, value4);

// Will output RenderScript: Here is some text! ... in Logcat
```

It is necessary to enter at least two arguments, the first one being the message and the remaining arguments values. All available `rsDebug` functions can be seen in the `api/rs_debug.spec`[178] source code file.

Random numbers

If you need to get a random number, you can use the `rsRand` function:

```
// Float version
float myNumber = rsRand(minValue, maxValue);

// Int version
int myIntNumber = rsRand(minValue, maxValue);
```

Blur

It is possible to blur Allocation contents using the `ScriptIntrinsicBlur` RenderScript Class:

```
// Creates an allocation from a Bitmap
Allocation inputAllocation = Allocation.createFromBitmap(mRS, inputImage);

// Creates an output Allocation where to store the blur result
Type.Builder tbOutput = new Type.Builder(mRS, Element.RGBA_8888(mRS));
tbOutput.setX(inputImage.getWidth());
tbOutput.setY(inputImage.getHeight());
Allocation outputAllocation = Allocation.createTyped(mRS, tbOutput.create());

// Instantiates the blur script
ScriptIntrinsicBlur blurScript = ScriptIntrinsicBlur.create(mRS, Element.U8(mRS));

// Sets the blur radius (pixels)
blurScript.setRadius(5);

// Compute the blurred allocation
blur.setInput(inputAllocation);
blur.forEach(outputAllocation);
```

---

[178] RenderScript source code - `api/rs_debug.spec` - https://android.googlesource.com/platform/frameworks/rs/+/marshmallow-mr1-release/api/rs_debug.spec

YUV to RGBA conversion

If you capture an image from Android Camera, the output will be a YUV NV21[179] image. You can convert it to an RGBA image (so that you can access the pixels content inside an allocation), where the A (alpha channel) will always be 255 (always opaque).

The input allocation needs to be prepared accordingly to the YUV type. This can be done in, at least, two ways:

> Using the `Element.DataKind.PIXEL_YUV` attribute:

```java
Type.Builder yuvTypeBuilder = new Type.Builder(mRS, Element.createPixel(mRS,
                              Element.DataType.UNSIGNED_8, Element.DataKind.PIXEL_YUV));
yuvTypeBuilder.setX(inputImageSize.x);
yuvTypeBuilder.setY(inputImageSize.y);
yuvTypeBuilder.setYuvFormat(android.graphics.ImageFormat.NV21);
Type yuvType = yuvTypeBuilder.create();
Allocation inputAllocation = Allocation.createTyped(mRS, yuvType, Allocation.USAGE_SCRIPT);
```

> Using a raw YUV type:

```java
// Calculates the expected YUV bytes count as YUV is not a human friendly
// way of storing data:
// https://en.wikipedia.org/wiki/YUV
//                       #Y.27UV420p_.28and_Y.27V12_or_YV12.29_to_RGB888_conversion
int expectedBytes = inputImageSize.x * inputImageSize.y *
                                ImageFormat.getBitsPerPixel(ImageFormat.NV21) / 8;

Type.Builder yuvTypeBuilder = new Type.Builder(mRS, Element.U8(mRS)).setX(expectedBytes);
Type yuvType = yuvTypeBuilder.create();
Allocation inputAllocation = Allocation.createTyped(mRS, yuvType, Allocation.USAGE_SCRIPT);
```

The conversion process can be achieved using at least two different ways:

> `ScriptIntrinsicYuvToRGB` class, which is a Script already built inside RenderScript, that works in this way:

```java
// Creates temporary allocation that will match camera preview size
Type.Builder rgbaType = new Type.Builder(mRS, Element.RGBA_8888(mRS))
rgbaType.setX(mInputImageSize.x);
rgbaType.setY(mInputImageSize.y);
Allocation outputAllocation = Allocation.createTyped(mRS,  rgbaType.create(),
                                                     Allocation.USAGE_SCRIPT);

// Creates conversion script
ScriptIntrinsicYuvToRGB sYUV = ScriptIntrinsicYuvToRGB.create(mRS, Element.U8_4(mRS));

sYUV.setInput(inputAllocation);

// Does the conversion
sYUV.forEach(outputAllocation);
```

> Custom YUV to RGBA converter script: You can find an example of it in our CameraCaptureExample sample project[180]. Look for the useCustomYUVToRGBConversion boolean in RSCompute.java file, to toggle it.

The full RenderScript code is as follows:

```
rs_allocation inputAllocation;

int wIn, hIn;
int numTotalPixels;

// Function to invoke before applying conversion
void setInputImageSize(int _w, int _h)
{
    wIn = _w;
    hIn = _h;
    numTotalPixels = wIn * hIn;
}

// Kernel that converts a YUV element to a RGBA one
uchar4 __attribute__((kernel)) convert(uint32_t x, uint32_t y)
{

    // YUV 4:2:0 planar image, with 8 bit Y samples, followed by
    // interleaved V/U plane with 8bit 2x2 subsampled chroma samples
    int baseIdx = x + y * wIn;
    int baseUYIndex = numTotalPixels + (y >> 1) * wIn + (x & 0xfffffe);

    uchar _y = rsGetElementAt_uchar(inputAllocation, baseIdx);
    uchar _u = rsGetElementAt_uchar(inputAllocation, baseUYIndex);
    uchar _v = rsGetElementAt_uchar(inputAllocation, baseUYIndex + 1);
    _y = _y < 16 ? 16 : _y;

    short Y = ((short)_y) - 16;
    short U = ((short)_u) - 128;
    short V = ((short)_v) - 128;

    uchar4 out;
    out.r = (uchar) clamp((float)(
        (Y * 298 + V * 409 + 128) >> 8), 0, 255);
    out.g = (uchar) clamp((float)(
        (Y * 298 - U * 100 - V * 208 + 128) >> 8), 0, 255);
    out.b = (uchar) clamp((float)(
        (Y * 298 + U * 516 + 128) >> 8), 0, 255);
    out.a = 255;

    return out;
}
```

---

[180] CameraCaptureExample sample project - https://bitbucket.org/cmaster11/rsbookexamples/src/tip/CameraCaptureExample/

RGBA to grayscale conversion

If you need to convert an RGBA image to a grayscale one, you have to convert every pixel's value to its corresponding gray one.

The gray value is the sum of each channel luminance, which can be calculated using the NTSC formula[181]:

```
uchar grayValue = (float) pixel.r * 0.299f + (float) pixel.g * 0.587f + (float) pixel.b * 0.144f;
```

Another way of packing this multiplication is by creating a multiplier vector:

```
const static float3 toGray = {0.299f, 0.587f, 0.114f};
```

The conversion from RGBA to gray can depend upon two scenarios:

> If you need to convert an RGBA image to a multi-channel one (another RGBA image, e.g. for displaying a bitmap), you can use the following implementation:

```
// Assume that the input is given by variable: uchar4 in
// Assume that the output is an uchar4

// Unpacks uchar4 to float4. Output values ranges from 0.0 to 1.0.
float4 pixel = rsUnpackColor8888(in);

// Performs dot multiplication over rgb values
// pixel.rgb returns a float3 composed by r, g and b values
float4 fGrayScale = dot(pixel.rgb, toGray);

// Packs float4 to uchar4, multiplying each value by 255
uchar4 grayScale = rsPackColorTo8888(fGrayScale);

return grayScale;
```

> If you need to convert the image to a single channel one, the following can be used:

```
// Assume that the input is given by variable: uchar4 in
// Assume that the output is a uchar
uchar out = (uchar) rsClamp(
    ((float)in.r * toGray.r) +
    ((float)in.g * toGray.g) +
    ((float)in.b * toGray.b),
        0.0f, 255.0f);

return out;
```

You can find an example of an RGBA to gray conversion in our ExampleRGBAToGray sample project[182].

---

[181] NTSC formula - Image and Video Compression for Multimedia Engineering: Fundamentals, Algorithms, and Standards, Second Edition - By Yun Q. Shi, Huifang Sun (2008) - http://dl.acm.org/citation.cfm?id=1796354
[182] ExampleRGBAToGray sample project - https://bitbucket.org/cmaster11/rsbookexamples/src/tip/ExampleRGBAToGray/

Surface rendering

You can draw on surfaces, you know? Android provides two classes that can be used to achieve this goal: `SurfaceView` and `TextureView`.

You can find an example of this process, which uses a `SurfaceView` component, inside the SurfaceRenderExample sample project[183].

SurfaceView
Android provides the `SurfaceView` class, defined[184] as:

> *Provides a dedicated drawing surface embedded inside of a view hierarchy. You can control the format of this surface and, if you like, its size; the SurfaceView takes care of placing the surface at the correct location on the screen.*

TextureView
Android provides the `TextureView` class, defined[185] as:

> *A TextureView can be used to display a content stream. Such a content stream can for instance be a video or an OpenGL scene. The content stream can come from the application's process as well as a remote process.*

Usage

You can use a `SurfaceView` or `TextureView` to display the content of an Allocation, which needs to be instantiated with:

> Element RGBA_8888 (which is the same as U8_4, but requires to be written in this way).
> USAGE_IO_OUTPUT usage flag, that tells RenderScript that it will be used to provide data to a surface.

Example:

```java
// Defines the output allocation type. You need ot impose the
// RGBA_8888 element (equal to U8_4)
Type.Builder tb = new Type.Builder(mRS, Element.RGBA_8888(mRS));
tb.setX(renderAllocationWidth);
tb.setY(renderAllocationHeight);
// Instantiates the output allocation, using the USAGE_IO_OUTPUT
// flag because it will give its data to the surface
renderAllocation = Allocation.createTyped(mRS, tb.create(), Allocation.USAGE_SCRIPT |
                                                    Allocation.USAGE_IO_OUTPUT);
```

To display an Allocation content, the workflow to follow is:

> Instantiate the `SurfaceView` or `TextureView`.
> Wait for it to become initialized, using a `SurfaceHolder.Callback`/`TextureView.SurfaceTextureListener` callback.
> Set the `SurfaceHolder`/`SurfaceTexture` object, which was given inside the initialization callback, as your Allocation's output surface:

>> When you have to deal with a `SurfaceView` class, you can set its result in this way:

```java
SurfaceHolder.Callback mSurfaceViewCallback =
    new SurfaceHolder.Callback() {
        @Override
        public void surfaceCreated(SurfaceHolder holder) {
            Surface surface = holder.getSurface();

            // Pass the surface to RenderScript
```

---

[183] SurfaceRenderExample sample project - https://bitbucket.org/cmaster11/rsbookexamples/src/tip/SurfaceRenderExample/
[184] SurfaceView - Android developers - http://developer.android.com/reference/android/view/SurfaceView.html
[185] TextureView - Android developers - http://developer.android.com/reference/android/view/TextureView.html

```
renderAllocation.setSurface(surface);
...
```

» When you have to deal with a `TextureView` class, you can set its result in this way:

```java
TextureView.SurfaceTextureListener mSurfaceTextureListener =
    new TextureView.SurfaceTextureListener() {
        @Override
        public void onSurfaceTextureAvailable(SurfaceTexture surface, int width, int height) {
            Surface mSurface = new Surface(surface);

            // Pass the surface to RenderScript
            renderAllocation.setSurface(mSurface);
            ...
```

> Do your calculations.
> Flush your Allocation content to the surface using the `Allocation.ioSend()` method.

Note: an important thing to keep in mind when dealing with surfaces, render-time drawing or endless drawing loops, is to use a separate thread to perform RenderScript activities:

```java
Thread rsLoop = new Thread(new Runnable() {
    boolean mbCanRun = true;

    @Override
    public void run() {
        while (mbCanRun) {
        // Perform RenderScript calculations
        ...

        // Sends output allocation to surface
        renderAllocation.ioSend();
        }
    }
...

// Start the rendering loop
rsLoop.start();
```

Workflow

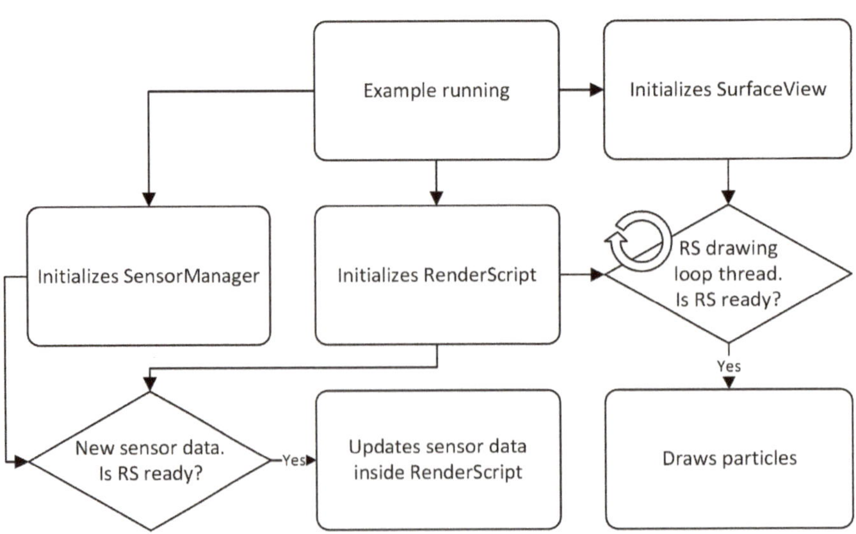

SurfaceRenderExample working diagram

Camera capture

Do you want to capture your camera image and perform some transformations over it?

You can follow our CameraCaptureExample sample project[186], which was made exactly for this purpose. Here is an explanation of its process:

1. Instantiate the camera preview surface (in this example I'm using a SurfaceView to show you all the possible combinations of surfaces usage), which will display current camera image in real-time mode.
2. Wait for the preview surface to be initialized with a SurfaceHolder.Callback.
3. Open the camera, set all the required parameters (maximum preview size, orientation, etc…) and initialize RenderScript Allocations (you need to know the size of the camera image you will get as input, that's why you have to wait for the camera initialization), both input and output ones.
4. On each camera frame, start RenderScript computation (if and only if output TextureView has initialized).

Note: this example still uses the deprecated Camera[187] class, because the new camera2[188] one does not provide support for API versions lower than 21.

Workflow

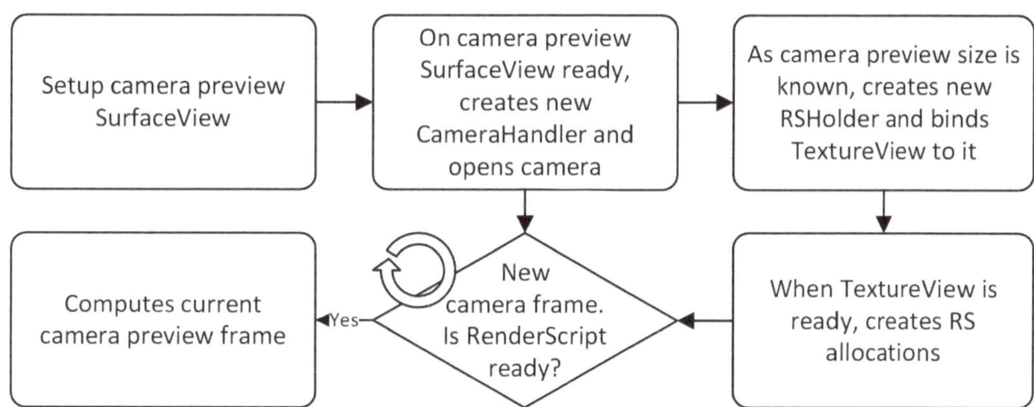

CameraCaptureExample working diagram

The project is divided into the following classes:

MainActivity
Orchestrates the entire process. Manages the initialization of the SurfaceView component.

CameraHandler
Used to open the Camera and set it up.

RSCompute
Used to perform all RenderScript calculations. Also, manages the initialization of the TextureView component.

Note: if you ever receive the error java.lang.RuntimeException: Fail to connect to camera service, be sure to add the following row into your AndroidManifest.xml file, under the manifest section:

```
<uses-permission android:name="android.permission.CAMERA" />
```

---

[186] CameraCaptureExample sample project - https://bitbucket.org/cmaster11/rsbookexamples/src/tip/CameraCaptureExample/
[187] Camera - Android Developers - http://developer.android.com/reference/android/hardware/Camera.html
[188] camera2 - Android Developers - http://developer.android.com/reference/android/hardware/camera2/package-summary.html

Profiling code

In case you need to profile RenderScript code (keep track of calculation times for debug purposes), using **Android Device Monitor** may not be suitable for repeated processes. You can, however, calculate the average time elapsed using simple formulas:

```
time0 = Current time (milliseconds)

myScript.forEach_myKernel(...);
mRS.finish(); // Waits for kernel to end

time1 = Current time - time0 = Elapsed time
```

Doing this process over a good amount of observations (>= 10) and calculating the average elapsed time can give you a good idea of actual computation time.

You can find an example of this in the ProfilerExample sample project[189], wherein a custom `Timings` class is used, which handles all the calculations (and that you can reuse if you want to!).

Resizing images

When you need to resize an image, you can use multiple approaches:

> Using `ScriptIntrinsicResize` class (min API 20).
> Using a custom implementation.

Custom implementation

Note: the following code can be found in the ImageResizeExample sample project[190].

It all starts by analyzing input and output image sizes.

RenderScript data is as follows:

```
// Sets image sizes and calculates the scale factor
static float scaleInv;
static int inputWidth, inputHeight, outputWidth, outputHeight;

void setInformation(int _inputWidth, int _inputHeight,
    int _outputWidth, int _outputHeight){

    inputWidth = _inputWidth;
    inputHeight = _inputHeight;
    outputWidth = _outputWidth;
    outputHeight = _outputHeight;

    // Calculates inverse scale factor, by which
    // to round coordinates.
    //
    // Ex:
    // Input size is 100
    // Output desired size is 25
    //
    // Scale factor is 25 / 100 = 0.25
    // Inverse scale factor is 1 / 0.25 = 4
    //
    // When iterating directly on the output
```

---

[189] ProfilerExample sample project - https://bitbucket.org/cmaster11/rsbookexamples/src/tip/ProfilerExample/
[190] ImageResizeExample sample project - https://bitbucket.org/cmaster11/rsbookexamples/src/tip/ImageResizeExample/

```
    // allocation, it is needed to use the inverse scale
    // factor to get the corresponding input element.
    //
    // Current output element index is 20
    // Respective input element index is 20 * 4 = 80
    //
    scaleInv = (float)inputWidth/(float)outputWidth;
}
```

The setInformation function can be invoked on the Java side using the following line of code:

```
main.invoke_setInformation(inputWidth, inputHeight, outputWidth, outputHeight);
```

In the sample project, two common resizing methods are implemented:

> Nearest neighbor[191] resize, which copies a single input pixel, approximating its x and y coordinates by rounding the multiplication between initial coordinates and scale factor:

```
uchar4 __attribute__((kernel)) resizeNearest(uint32_t x, uint32_t y) {

    float fX = clamp((float)x*scaleInv, 0.0f, inputWidth);
    float fY = clamp((float)y*scaleInv, 0.0f, inputHeight);

    return rsGetElementAt_uchar4(inputAllocation, fX, fY);
}
```

> Bicubic interpolation[192] resize, which creates a new pixel by interpolating neighbor data. This implementation has been directly ported from Google RenderScript examples[193].

---

191 Nearest neighbor interpolation - Wikipedia - https://en.wikipedia.org/wiki/Nearest-neighbor_interpolation
192 Bicubic interpolation - Wikipedia - https://en.wikipedia.org/wiki/Bicubic_interpolation
193 Google RenderScript examples - https://android.googlesource.com/platform/frameworks/rs/+/marshmallow-mr1-release/java/tests/ImageProcessing2/src/com/android/rs/image/resize.rs

Color normalization

There are some cases when image colors have to be normalized[194], like when you have to deal with color-based object recognition. In our ColorNormalizationExample sample project[195], you can see a simple normalization of an image.

By normalizing an image, colors get equalized, so that shades and tints[196] are converted to tones:

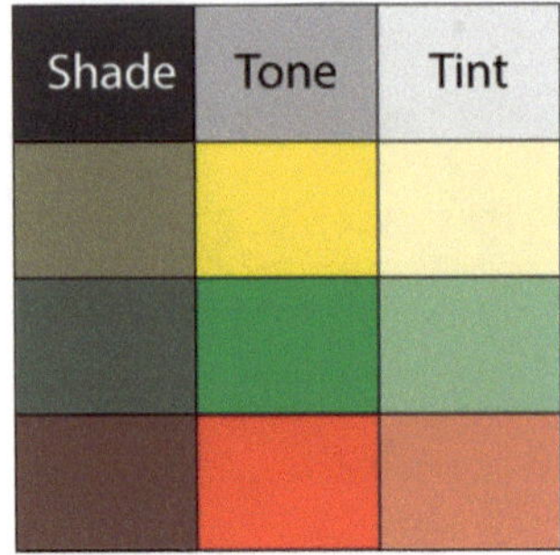

Shades, tones and tints

I'm using the following kernel:

```c
uchar4 __attribute__((kernel)) normalizeImage(uchar4 in, int x, int y){

    // Converts uchars to floats. fIn values range from 0.0 to 1.0 inclusive.
    float4 fIn = rsUnpackColor8888(in);

    // Creates sum of color for current pixel
    float sum = fIn.r + fIn.g + fIn.b;

    float4 fOut;
    fOut.a = 1.0f;

    // Calculates weighted divisions of pixel channels
    fOut.r = fIn.r / sum;
    fOut.g = fIn.g / sum;
    fOut.b = fIn.b / sum;

    // Converts to uchar values. Multiplies each float by 255
    uchar4 out = rsPackColorTo8888(fOut);

    return out;

}
```

---

194 Color normalization - Wikipedia - https://en.wikipedia.org/wiki/Color_normalization
195 ColorNormalizationExample sample project -
https://bitbucket.org/cmaster11/rsbookexamples/src/tip/ColorNormalizationExample/
196 Tints and shades - Wikipedia - https://en.wikipedia.org/wiki/Tints_and_shades

Custom struct element copy to Java

Disclaimer: the following example should be used only for debug purposes, because this approach is slow and does not have certain compatibility with RenderScript API.

The CustomStructElementCopyToJava sample project[197] is an example of the following described process.

When instantiating a *custom struct element*-based allocation in RenderScript, there is for now (API 23) no direct way to copy its data to its Java wrapper class.

Let's assume using the following custom struct element:

```
typedef struct __attribute__((packed, aligned(4))) GrayPoint {
    short a;
    int x;
    int y;
    char b;
} GrayPoint_t;
```

When looking at the generated code of the struct (which can be seen, in Android Studio, by pressing **CTRL+B** while focusing on a `ScriptField_GrayPoint` element on the Java side), the following elements can be seen:

> A `Item.sizeof` integer variable, having a value of 16 (bytes), defines how much space is occupied by a single GrayPoint_t struct element.

> The `createElement` function defines what is occupying those 16 bytes:

```
public static Element createElement(RenderScript rs) {
    Element.Builder eb = new Element.Builder(rs);
    eb.add(Element.I16(rs), "a");
    eb.add(Element.U16(rs), "#rs_padding_1");
    eb.add(Element.I32(rs), "x");
    eb.add(Element.I32(rs), "y");
    eb.add(Element.I8(rs), "b");
    eb.add(Element.U16(rs), "#rs_padding_2");
    eb.add(Element.U8(rs), "#rs_padding_3");
    return eb.create();
}
```

Padding

#rs_padding_* elements exist because of a classic problem, data structure alignment[198]. Aligning elements to memory can give benefits in terms of performance (e.g. see StackOverflow's *Bit Aligning for Space and Performance Boosts*[199] discussion).

The following process has already been described (on different topic), inside the *RenderScript and NDK - mallocPtr member* chapter.

In the struct, the biggest elements are x or y, both having a size of 4 bytes. The *slang compiler* will then refer to this size as the biggest one and align, in memory, every member to it.

> #rs_padding_1 exists because the a element is just 2 bytes big. To fill the gap in memory, to reach the next element (which is 4 bytes long), a padding of 2 bytes is needed.

> #rs_padding_2 and #rs_padding_3 paddings exist because the total size of the struct must be a multiple of the biggest element size: with these, the struct's size becomes 16 bytes, instead of 13.

---

[197] CustomStructElementCopyToJava sample project - https://bitbucket.org/cmaster11/rsbookexamples/src/tip/CustomStructElementCopyToJava/
[198] Data structure alignment - Wikipedia - https://en.wikipedia.org/wiki/Data_structure_alignment
[199] StackOverflow - Bit Aligning for Space and Performance Boosts - http://stackoverflow.com/questions/9086656/bit-aligning-for-space-and-performance-boosts

There are two ways to delete these paddings:

1. Changing the struct elements' order, from biggest to smallest. One way is to use the following struct definition:

```c
typedef struct __attribute__((packed)) GrayPointOrdered {
    int x;
    int y;
    short a;
    char b;
} GrayPointOrdered_t;
```

The code generated is:

```java
public static final int sizeof = 12;
...
public static Element createElement(RenderScript rs) {
    Element.Builder eb = new Element.Builder(rs);
    eb.add(Element.I32(rs), "x");
    eb.add(Element.I32(rs), "y");
    eb.add(Element.I16(rs), "a");
    eb.add(Element.I8(rs), "b");
    eb.add(Element.U8(rs), "#rs_padding_1");
    return eb.create();
}
```

The total size has been reduced to 11 bytes, and only 1 byte padding is then needed to get a multiple of 4 bytes.

2. Using the packed attribute, with the following definition:

```c
typedef struct __attribute__((packed)) GrayPointPacked {
    ushort a;
    uint x;
    uint y;
    uchar b;
} GrayPointPacked_t;
```

The code generated is:

```java
public static final int sizeof = 11;
...
public static Element createElement(RenderScript rs) {
    Element.Builder eb = new Element.Builder(rs);
    eb.add(Element.I16(rs), "a");
    eb.add(Element.I32(rs), "x");
    eb.add(Element.I32(rs), "y");
    eb.add(Element.I8(rs), "b");
    return eb.create();
}
```

The packed attribute tells the compiler that all struct elements should be contiguous. This, however, can generate some problems when using pointers, because memory addresses could be masked by the packing (e.g. see StackOverflow's *Does GCC's __attribute__((__packed__))...?*[200] discussion).

The best behavior is obtained when elements are correctly ordered in memory.

---

[200] StackOverflow - Does GCC's __attribute__((__packed__))...? - http://stackoverflow.com/a/7956942/3671330

Offset

Let's use the `GrayPointOrdered_t` struct type, and recap on its properties.

The offset (location in memory) of its elements is:

Element	Size (bytes)	Offset (bytes)
x	4	+ 0
y	4	+ 4
a	2	+ 8
b	1	+ 10
#rs_padding_1	1	+ 11
Total	**12**	

For example, given a void * pointer to an element, the a member could be accessed (in a C-like language) by using `*(int16_t*)(pointer + 8)`.

Reading elements

On the Java side, it is possible to use the `ScriptField_GrayPointOrdered.Item` class to map the RS struct. To read all elements, the `Allocation.copyTo` method can be used. However, its standard implementation has a limitation.

The process required is:

1. Copy all Allocation contents to a byte array (each element having a size of 1 byte).
2. Use the ByteBuffer[201] class to map array contents into custom struct elements.

Allocation contents copy

First of all, it is necessary to copy the entire Allocation contents. Usually, what could be done is to use directly the `Allocation.copyTo` function:

```java
byte destinationArray[] = new byte[allocationGrayPointOrdered.getBytesSize()];

allocationGrayPointOrdered.copyTo(destinationArray);
```

However, this cannot be done in this case: `Allocation.copyTo` function's implementation contains a check:

```java
public void copyTo(byte[] d) {
    validateIsInt8();
    copyTo(d, Element.DataType.SIGNED_8, d.length);
}
```

`validateIsInt8()` function checks that the source Allocation base element is a `SIGNED_8` or `UNSIGNED_8`.

It is then necessary to call directly the `copyTo` function, bypassing the validation.

---

[201] ByteBuffer - Oracle - https://docs.oracle.com/javase/7/docs/api/java/nio/ByteBuffer.html

Reflection method

To bypass the validation, the `Allocation.copyTo` method has to be mapped:

```java
private static Method getCopyToWithoutValidationMethod(){
    // private void copyTo(Object array, Element.DataType dt, int arrayLen)
    Method allocationHiddenCopyToMethod = null;
    try {
        allocationHiddenCopyToMethod =
            Allocation.class.getDeclaredMethod("copyTo", Object.class,
                                        Element.DataType.class, int.class);

        allocationHiddenCopyToMethod.setAccessible(true);
    } catch (NoSuchMethodException e) {
        throw new RuntimeException("Could not find allocationHiddenCopyToMethod");
    }

    return allocationHiddenCopyToMethod;
}
```

Contents copy

The mapped method can then be used to copy the contents:

```java
//--- Copy process
// Define the destination array
byte destinationArray[] = new byte[allocationGrayPointOrdered.getBytesSize()];

// Gets reflected method
Method copyToWithoutValidationMethod = getCopyToWithoutValidationMethod();

// Tries to copy contents
try {
    copyToWithoutValidationMethod.invoke(allocationGrayPointOrdered, destinationArray,
                                Element.DataType.UNSIGNED_8, destinationArray.length);
} catch (IllegalAccessException e) {
    throw new RuntimeException(e);
} catch (InvocationTargetException e) {
    throw new RuntimeException(e);
}
```

Contents mapping

Once the array is filled with source data, it is then possible to map its content to a human-readable struct.

```java
// Defines the destination array
ScriptField_GrayPointOrdered.Item mappedItems[][] =
                                new ScriptField_GrayPointOrdered.Item[sizeX][sizeY];

// Wraps array contents
ByteBuffer byteBuffer = ByteBuffer.wrap(destinationArray);
// Sets byte order to be Android-like
byteBuffer.order(ByteOrder.LITTLE_ENDIAN);

// Iterates on every column and row
for (int x = 0; x < sizeX; x++) {
    for (int y = 0; y < sizeY; y++) {

        // Allocates a new item
        ScriptField_GrayPointOrdered.Item currentItem = new ScriptField_GrayPointOrdered.Item();

        // Calculate the offset in the source array
        int currentOffset = (x + y * sizeX) * ScriptField_GrayPointOrdered.Item.sizeof;
```

```java
        // Gets data from the byte array
        currentItem.x = byteBuffer.getInt(currentOffset);
        currentItem.y = byteBuffer.getInt(currentOffset + 4);
        currentItem.a = byteBuffer.getShort(currentOffset + 8);
        currentItem.b = byteBuffer.get(currentOffset + 10);

        mappedItems[x][y] = currentItem;
    }
}
```

Debugging elements

Once the copy is done, to test the process, simple debug functions can be used on both sides:

RenderScript

```c
void debugElements(rs_allocation inputAllocation,
    int sizeX, int sizeY){
    for (int x = 0; x < sizeX; x++) {
        for (int y = 0; y < sizeY; y++) {
            GrayPointOrdered_t item = * (GrayPointOrdered_t *) rsGetElementAt(inputAllocation, x, y);

            rsDebug("Element", x, y, item.a, item.b);
        }
    }
}
```

Java

```java
for (int x = 0; x < sizeX; x++) {
    for (int y = 0; y < sizeY; y++) {
        ScriptField_GrayPointOrdered.Item item = mappedItems[x][y];
        Log.d(TAG, String.format("(%d,%d): x=%d, y=%d, a=%d, b=%d",
                                        x, y, item.x, item.y, item.a, item.b));
    }
}
```

Output

If everything works fine, a result of the debugging can be:

```
D/RenderScript: ... {0.000000, 0.000000, 27530.000000, 50.000000}
D/RenderScript: ... {0.000000, 1.000000, 10984.000000, 97.000000}
D/RenderScript: ... {1.000000, 0.000000, 25659.000000, 101.000000}
D/RenderScript: ... {1.000000, 1.000000, 9101.000000, 70.000000}
D/RenderScript: ... {2.000000, 0.000000, 29871.000000, 25.000000}
D/RenderScript: ... {2.000000, 1.000000, 15642.000000, 79.000000}
D/Java: (0,0): x=0, y=0, a=27530, b=50
D/Java: (0,1): x=0, y=1, a=10984, b=97
D/Java: (1,0): x=1, y=0, a=25659, b=101
D/Java: (1,1): x=1, y=1, a=9101, b=70
D/Java: (2,0): x=2, y=0, a=29871, b=25
D/Java: (2,1): x=2, y=1, a=15642, b=79
```

Dynamic bitcode loading

Compiled RenderScript scripts are stored as bitcode[202] files, loaded at runtime inside Android applications. This loading process, for standard applications (created with Android Studio), is usually hidden because reflection files are generated automatically to invoke RS kernels and set variables.

However, it is possible to manually/programmatically perform this loading task by using Reflection methods and accessing native RS classes and elements. In the DynamicBitcodeLoaderExample sample project[203] a stub of infrastructure that can be used to perform this task is provided.

Note: this example could be used to create a daily-updated self-updating app, or to create a distributed calculation system that uses mobile-related inputs (camera, sensors) to provide data to back-end systems.

To test this example:

> Inside the `rslibrary` module, observe the RS file `computeThreshold.rs`.
> Build the `rslibrary` module, and observe that a `.zip` file and a `.properties` file have been generated inside the `rslibrary/build/bitcodes` folder.
> Upload this `.zip` file to a remote server, or just use the default remote pre-built archive, located at http://hydex11.net/rsbook/dynscripts/computethreshold.zip.
> Set your remote server URL inside the `remoteUrl` variable of the app -> `ScriptDownloader.java` file.
> Run the app project and watch the script working!

Workflow

The diagram below explains how this example works:

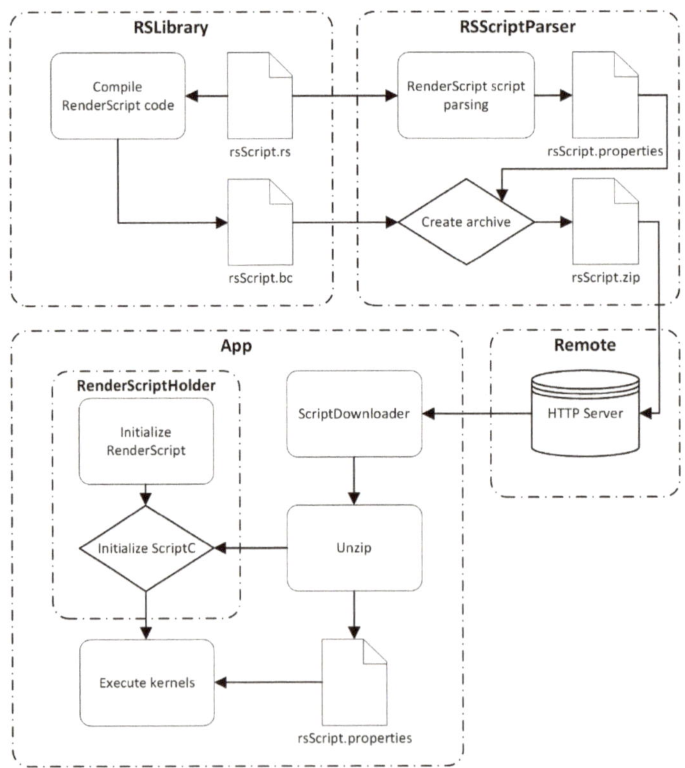

Dynamic bitcode loading example working diagram

---

[202] Bitcode - LLVM.org - http://llvm.org/docs/BitCodeFormat.html
[203] DynamicBitcodeLoaderExample sample project - https://bitbucket.org/cmaster11/rsbookexamples/src/tip/DynamicBitcodeLoaderExample/

Module - rsscriptparser

The `rsscriptparser` library does the following process, for every `.rs` or `.fs` file it finds:

> Checks that a corresponding `.bc` file exists for the current script. Otherwise, skips current script.
> Checks for text lines starting with a specific token (in the example, it is `//D`).
> Extracts previously matched lines and copies their contents to a `.properties` file, its name matching the script's one.
> Creates a `.zip` file, its file matching the script's one, containing both `.bc` and `.properties` files.

Module - rslibrary

The `rslibrary` module is used to create RS scripts and compile them.

You use some custom Gradle tasks that automate our processes:

```
// Just a sample task, in this case for debug build type.
// It copies the compiled bitcode files inside another directory
// to improve the project order.
task copyRSBitcode(type: Copy) {
    from('build/generated/res/rs/debug/raw')
    into("$projectDir/build/bitcodes")

    include '*.bc' // Copy bitcode files
}


// Invokes rsscriptparser library, which will generate .properties files,
// one for each RS script that was compiled to bc. It will check that, for
// any .rs file, the corresponding .bc file exists, before parsing it.
task parseRSScripts(dependsOn: copyRSBitcode,type: JavaExec) {

    main = 'net.hydex11.RSScriptParser'

    classpath files("$projectDir/../rsscriptparser/build/classes/main")

    args = [
        "$projectDir/src/main/rs",
        "$projectDir/build/bitcodes"
    ].toList()

}


// Here we tell Gradle that, when we invoke the assembleDebug task, it will be followed by
// our custom tasks.
assembleDebug.finalizedBy(parseRSScripts)
```

Whenever the module is built, `.zip` files are generated for each *.rs* file.

Note: after compilation and creation of the `.zip` file, it should be uploaded to a remote server (in the example, it gets uploaded to http://hydex11.net/rsbook/dynscripts/calculatethreshold.zip), so that it can be downloaded using the app module.

Module - app

This is the runtime Android application, which will download scripts, extract their `.zip` files, load bitcodes inside a RenderScript context and run the example.

It is composed of the following classes:

MainActivity
Orchestrates the entire process.

RenderScriptHolder
The job of this class is to access private RenderScript methods to manually instantiate scripts and invoke kernels.

ScriptDownloader
Used to download remote scripts.

Unzip
Unzips downloaded script archives.

Common
Various utility classes.

Porting case - FAST features detection

In this chapter I'll present a porting process, to let a user perform a certain action, usually achieved with the aid of a Java or C++ library, using RenderScript. Porting a library means converting its existing code to a RenderScript-compatible one.

The porting will be done to achieve FAST features detection, starting from two different C++ libraries.

The result of the following porting can be observed in the FASTExample sample project[204].

FAST features

In the Computer Vision[205] field, which has tons of different branches, one in particular is used by the augmented[206] and virtual[207] reality fields: detection of corners[208], edges[209] and blobs[210].

Corners, edges and blobs are also called **features**, as they preserve their informative content between different images: imagine that you are traveling by car along a really long road. On you left you have a mountain. You can understand that you are progressing on the road as you see the mountain shifting backwards. If you are traveling in a mist bank, you can not rely on any visual point to understand how you are actually moving. The mountain is a visual feature that your brain uses as a reference in the environment, which has the same meaning as corners, edges and blobs in computer vision.

Features extraction is achieved with two different steps: **detection** and **description**.

Detection
The detection process understands where, in an image, there are relevant points (called **keypoints**), which are going to be used as the base of our features.

Description
The description process grabs information from the surroundings of a point, to create a definition of it (a so called **descriptor**).

There are many kinds of features detectors[211] and extractors and here I talk about one of the fastest detectors, which can be reliably used on mobile phones, for real-time cases: **FAST**[212] corner detector.

---

[204] FASTExample sample project - https://bitbucket.org/cmaster11/rsbookexamples/src/tip/FASTExample/
[205] Computer Vision - Wikipedia - https://en.wikipedia.org/wiki/Computer_vision
[206] Augmented reality - Wikipedia - https://en.wikipedia.org/wiki/Augmented_reality
[207] Virtual reality - Wikipedia - https://en.wikipedia.org/wiki/Virtual_reality
[208] Corner detection - Wikipedia - https://en.wikipedia.org/wiki/Corner_detection
[209] Edge detection - Wikipedia - https://en.wikipedia.org/wiki/Edge_detection
[210] Blob detection - Wikipedia - https://en.wikipedia.org/wiki/Blob_detection
[211] Feature detection - Wikipedia - https://en.wikipedia.org/wiki/Feature_detection_(computer_vision)
[212] FAST features - Wikipedia - https://en.wikipedia.org/wiki/Features_from_accelerated_segment_test

Detection process

The FAST features detector was created by Edward Rosten, and its details can be found at its home page:
http://www.edwardrosten.com/work/fast.html.

A FAST detection algorithm works by applying to every pixel of the image the following criteria:

> Get the current pixel value (**assuming the image belongs to the grayscale domain, so that it has only one channel, composed by unsigned char values, which range from 0 to 255**).

> Get the values of neighbor pixels, which belong to a circular patch as shown in the following image:

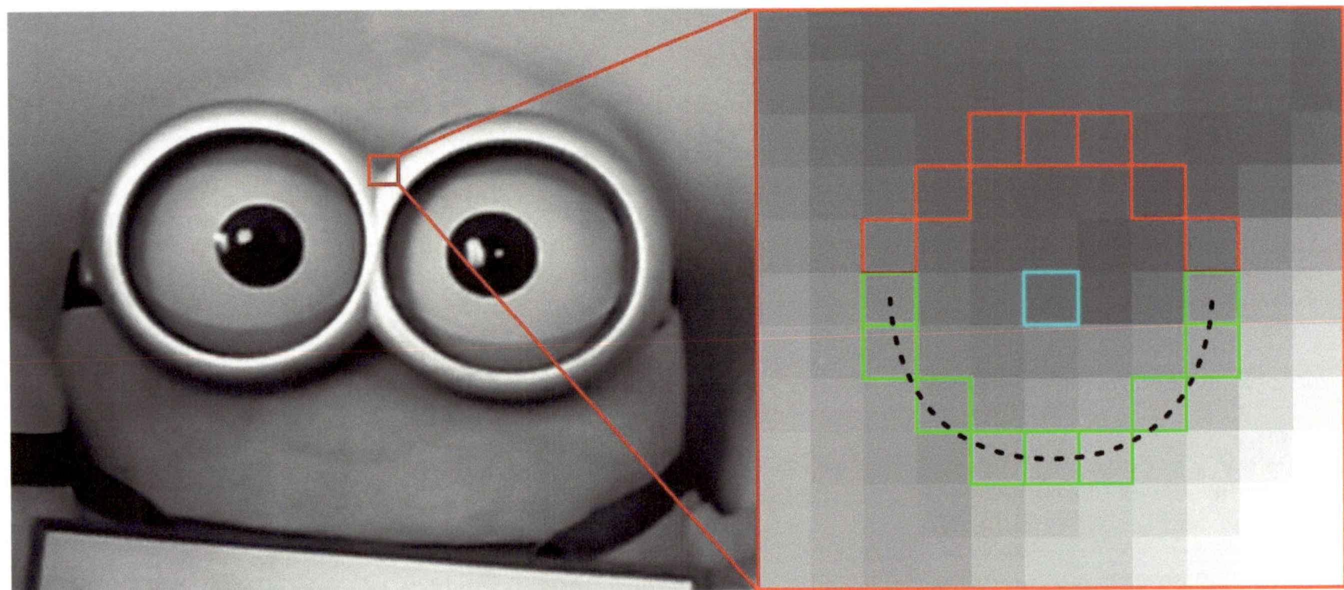

FAST corner, having 9 contiguous relevant pixels

> Sorting the point as shown in the image, if a sufficiently long sequence of them is much brighter or much darker then the central pixel, then the point is a FAST keypoint. The length of this sequence is usually 9 or 12. In the following example, a length of 9 will be used.

The porting process

Here comes the discussion about how the porting has been done, both for standard FAST library and OpenCV implementations. In the porting process, scoring functions (like fast9_score[213] and cornerScore[214]) will be skipped, because the scoring process can be done in different ways, as discussed *below*.

Input

The input must be assumed to be a grayscale image. The conversion to grayscale can be done following the code seen in the *YUV to RGB conversion* and *RGBA to grayscale conversion* examples.

Porting - Original FAST library

The porting of the original FAST library starts from its homepage[215], where its source code can be obtained. The file used as source, in this case, was the fast_9.c[216] one: it implements FAST extraction with a check for 9 contiguous points.

---

[213] FAST features source code - fast9_score - https://github.com/edrosten/fast-C-src/blob/master/fast_9.c#L2960
[214] OpenCV FAST features CUDA source code - cornerScore -
https://github.com/Itseez/opencv/blob/3.0.0/modules/cudafeatures2d/src/cuda/fast.cu#L195

Let's take a look at the source code. The general code structure is:

```c
static void make_offsets(...)
{
    ...
}

...

xy* fast9_detect(...)
{
    ...
    make_offsets(pixel, stride);
    ...
}
```

It all starts with the FAST detection function, fast9_detect[217], which has the following declaration:

```c
xy* fast9_detect(const byte* im, int xsize, int ysize, int stride, int b, int* ret_num_corners){ ... }
```

This function can be used over an entire image.

> xy is a simple struct, which will represent the coordinates of a found FAST point:

```c
typedef struct { int x, y; } xy;
```

> byte is a custom type, that ranges from 0 to 255:

```c
typedef unsigned char byte;
```

> im is the pointer to the first image pixel.
> xsize is the width of the input image and ysize its height.
> stride is the size, in bytes, of every image row. If the image is a grayscale one (only one channel), composed by unsigned char elements, the image stride will be equal to its width.
> b is the FAST threshold, which is used by the algorithm to compare neighbor pixels to the central one. This value can be set to 20 to achieve standard results (the same amount is used as default in the OpenCV library).
> ret_num_corners is the pointer to the variable that will contain the number of extracted keypoints, after the algorithm execution.

Let's assume the desired output of the porting to be a FilterScript implementation of the algorithm. This means that:

> No pointers can be used and the only available functions to retrieve and set values are rsGetElementAt and rsSetElementAt ones.
> The stride value becomes useless, because y values are directly accessed.
> The fastKpAllocation will store the keypoints. This means that there is no vector of keypoints, and no return value of the fast9_detect function. Instead, an image is used and, for each pixel, a value different from 0 means that, in a specific x-y coordinate, a FAST keypoint has been detected.

---

[215] FAST features - Edward Rosten - homepage - http://www.edwardrosten.com/work/fast.html
[216] FAST features source code - fast_9.c - https://github.com/edrosten/fast-C-src/blob/master/fast_9.c
[217] FAST features source code - fast9_detect - https://github.com/edrosten/fast-C-src/blob/master/fast_9.c#L2975

Function: `make_offsets`

First of all, the `make_offsets` function must be converted for our goal. Its job is to retrieve pixels of the circular patch using simple indices.

It gets called every time a pixel needs to be retrieved, `if(p[pixel[0]] > cb)`, p being the pointer to the current central pixel.

Its original source code is:

```c
static void make_offsets(int pixel[], int row_stride)
{
    pixel[0] = 0 + row_stride * 3;
    pixel[1] = 1 + row_stride * 3;
    ...
    pixel[14] = -2 + row_stride * 2;
    pixel[15] = -1 + row_stride * 3;
}
```

As the kernel created is going to be a FilterScript one, it will need to read from an allocation defined as script variable. The function can be easily converted this way:

```c
// This allocation contains the source image
rs_allocation grayAllocation;

static uchar getFASTPixel(uchar offset, int x, int y)
{
    switch(offset) {
    case 0:
        return rsGetElementAt_uchar(grayAllocation, x + 0 , y + 3);
        break;
    case 1:
        return rsGetElementAt_uchar(grayAllocation, x + 1 , y + 3);
        break;
    ...
    case 14:
        return rsGetElementAt_uchar(grayAllocation, x - 2 , y + 2);
        break;
    case 15:
        return rsGetElementAt_uchar(grayAllocation, x - 1, y + 3);
        break;
    ...
```

Now, the function can be called, for example, with the following invocation: `getFASTPixel(4, x, y)`.

Inner cycle limits

The inner cycle is defined this way:

```c
for(y=3; y < ysize - 3; y++)
    for(x=3; x < xsize - 3; x++)
```

It is necessary to force a limit over the execution of the process. This can be achieved on the Java side, instantiating a new `Script.LaunchOptions` element.

```java
Script.LaunchOptions fastLaunchOptions; = new Script.LaunchOptions();
fastLaunchOptions.setX(3, inputImageSize.width - 3);
fastLaunchOptions.setY(3, inputImageSize.height - 3);
```

The kernel

The relevant part of every iteration is the one that lies inside the main inner for cycle.

The main process, which is the FAST point detection, begins, in the original library, with the following code:

```
for(y=3; y < ysize - 3; y++)
    for(x=3; x < xsize - 3; x++)
    {
        // Here is the relevant part, which is going to
        // be ported inside a RS kernel
        const byte* p = im + y*stride + x;

        int cb = *p + b;
        int c_b= *p - b;

        if(p[pixel[0]] > cb)
            if(p[pixel[1]] > cb)
                if(p[pixel[2]] > cb)
                ...
                else
                    continue;
                ...
    }
```

> p, the current pixel, will be given as the argument of the RS kernel, so it is given without any needed invocation.
> b, the FAST threshold, can be set as a constant or script variable.
> cb and c_b can then be calculated directly.
> p[pixel[n]] instructions can be substituted by getFASTPixel(n, x, y) ones. A fast way to substitute them is by using the following regular expression[218]:

```
Search regex:    p\[pixel\[(\d+)\]\]      E.g.: p[pixel[2]]
Replace with:    getFASTPixel($1, x, y)   E.g.: getFASTPixel(2, x, y)
```

> continue instructions can, in our case, be converted directly to return 0, because that point will not be marked as a FAST keypoint.
> If the point gets detected as a FAST one, a return 1 instruction can be toggled at the end of the code.

The RenderScript kernel can then be defined in the following way:

```
const int fastThreshold = 20;
uchar __attribute__((kernel)) fastOptimized(uchar in, uint x, uint y)
{

    int cb = in + fastThreshold;
    int c_b = in - fastThreshold;

    if (getFASTPixel(0,x,y) > cb)
        if (getFASTPixel(1,x,y) > cb)
            if (getFASTPixel(2,x,y) > cb)
            ...
            else
                return 0;
            ...

    return 1;
}
```

---

[218] Regular expressions - Wikipedia - https://en.wikipedia.org/wiki/Regular_expression

Now, the kernel can be invoked, on the Java side. The required elements are:

> `grayAllocation`, which is the allocation containing the input grayscale image.
> `fastKpAllocation`, which is the allocation that will contain the algorithm results:
>> 0 if pixel is not a FAST keypoint.
>> 1 if pixel is a FAST keypoint.

Invocation can be done with the following code:

```
scriptCFast.forEach_fastOptimized(grayAllocation, fastKpAllocation, fastLaunchOptions);
```

Output allocation contents can be seen (in a Bitmap or *Surface*) using the following kernel function:

```
const uchar4 red = {255,0,0,255}; // RGBA
const uchar4 transparent = {0,0,0,0};
uchar4 __attribute__((kernel)) showFastKeypoints(uchar in, uint32_t x, uint32_t y)
{
    // If keypoint was found, displays a red point. Otherwise, transparent
    // pixel.
    if(in > 0) return red;
    return transparent;
}
```

Porting - OpenCV implementation

The OpenCV library offers a CUDA implementation[219] of the FAST features detector. The following one is the direct porting of this implementation.

The general code structure is:

```
namespace fast
{
    __device__ unsigned int g_counter = 0;

    //////////////////////////////////////////////////////////////////////////////////
    // calcKeypoints

    __constant__ uchar c_table[] = { ... }

    __device__ __forceinline__ int diffType(...)
    {
        ...
    }

    __device__ void calcMask(...)
    {
        ...
        d1 = diffType(v, C[0] & 0xff, th);
        ...
    }

    __device__ __forceinline__ bool isKeyPoint(...)
    {
        return (__popc(mask1) ...);
    }

    ...
```

---

[219] OpenCV FAST features CUDA implementation -
https://github.com/Itseez/opencv/blob/3.0.0/modules/cudafeatures2d/src/cuda/fast.cu

```cpp
template <bool calcScore, class Mask>
__global__ void calcKeypoints(...)
{
    ...
    int d1 = diffType(v, C[1] & 0xff, threshold);
    ...
    calcMask(C, v, threshold, mask1, mask2);
    ...
    if (isKeyPoint(mask1, mask2))
    ...
}


...
}
```

Constants

First of all, the c_table[220] constant can be copied and pasted in a header file (e.g. `fast_ctable.rsh`), that will be included later (the usage of an external header file is suggested because the size of the array can slow down some IDEs).

Its conversion can be done by changing

```cpp
__constant__ uchar c_table[] = { 0x80, 0x0, 0x0, ...
```

to

```cpp
static const uchar c_table[] = { 0x80, 0x0, 0x0, ...
```

Note: it's a good thing in this case to use the `static` keyword because, with it, the constant's data doesn't get reflected onto the Java side.

Function: `diffType`

The `diffType`[221] function can be converted directly from

```cpp
// 1 -> v > x + th
// 2 -> v < x - th
// 0 -> x - th <= v <= x + th
__device__ __forceinline__ int diffType(const int v, const int x, const int th)
{
    const int diff = x - v;
    return static_cast<int>(diff < -th) + (static_cast<int>(diff > th) << 1);
}
```

to

```cpp
static int diffType(const int v, const int x, const int th) {
    const int diff = x - v;
    return (diff < -th ? 1 : 0) + ((diff > th ? 1 : 0) << 1);
}
```

---

220 OpenCV FAST features CUDA source code - c_table -
https://github.com/Itseez/opencv/blob/3.0.0/modules/cudafeatures2d/src/cuda/fast.cu#L57
221 OpenCV FAST features CUDA source code - diffType -
https://github.com/Itseez/opencv/blob/3.0.0/modules/cudafeatures2d/src/cuda/fast.cu#L62

Function: `calcMask`

The calcMask[222] function has the following definition:

```cpp
__device__ void calcMask(const uint C[4], const int v, const int th, int& mask1, int& mask2)
{
    mask1 = 0;
    mask2 = 0;
    ...

    int d1, d2;

    d1 = diffType(v, C[0] & 0xff, th);
    d2 = diffType(v, C[2] & 0xff, th);
    ...

    d1 = diffType(v, C[1] & 0xff, th);
    d2 = diffType(v, C[3] & 0xff, th);
    ...
}
```

> It uses pointers to return mask1 and mask2 values. You can pack the return value in an `int2` struct.
> It uses a const array, `uint C[4]`. You can pack it in an `int4` struct.

Its conversion needs then to return an `int2` that will pack both mask1 and mask2 results:

```cpp
static int2 calcMask(const uint4 C, const int v, const int th)
{
    int2 mask;

    mask.x = 0; // Substitute every mask1 with mask.x
    mask.y = 0; // Substitute every mask2 with mask.y

    int d1, d2;

    d1 = diffType(v, C.x & 0xff, th); // Subst. every C[0] with C.x
    d2 = diffType(v, C.z & 0xff, th); // Subst. every C[2] with C.z
    ...

    d1 = diffType(v, C.y & 0xff, th); // Subst. every C[1] with C.y
    d2 = diffType(v, C.w & 0xff, th); // Subst. every C[3] with C.w
    ...

    return mask; // Added at end of function
}
```

Function: `isKeyPoint`

The isKeyPoint[223] function has the following implementation:

```cpp
__device__ __forceinline__ bool isKeyPoint(int mask1, int mask2)
{
    return (__popc(mask1) > 8 && (c_table[(mask1 >> 3) - 63] & (1 << (mask1 & 7)))) ||
           (__popc(mask2) > 8 && (c_table[(mask2 >> 3) - 63] & (1 << (mask2 & 7))));
}
```

---

[222] OpenCV FAST features CUDA source code - `calcMask` -
https://github.com/Itseez/opencv/blob/3.0.0/modules/cudafeatures2d/src/cuda/fast.cu#L69
[223] OpenCV FAST features CUDA source code - `isKeyPoint` -
https://github.com/Itseez/opencv/blob/3.0.0/modules/cudafeatures2d/src/cuda/fast.cu#L189

> It makes use of the `__popc`[224] intrisic CUDA function, used to calculate the Hamming Weight[225] of the variable (number of bits set to 1). A simple solution to recreate its behavior is to use the following function[226]:

```
static uint32_t __popc(uint32_t i){
    i = i - ((i >> 1) & 0x55555555);
    i = (i & 0x33333333) + ((i >> 2) & 0x33333333);
    return (((i + (i >> 4)) & 0x0F0F0F0F) * 0x01010101) >> 24;
}
```

> Earlier, the `mask1` and `mask2` variables had been packed to an `int2` one.

The ported code looks like this:

```
static bool isKeyPoint(int2 mask) {
    return (__popc(mask.x) > 8 && (c_table[(mask.x >> 3) - 63] & (1 << (mask.x & 7)))) ||
           (__popc(mask.y) > 8 && (c_table[(mask.y >> 3) - 63] & (1 << (mask.y & 7)))));
}
```

Function: `calcKeypoints`

`calcKeypoints`[227] is the kernel function that orchestrates the entire process. Its source code is as follows:

```
template <bool calcScore, class Mask>
__global__ void calcKeypoints(const PtrStepSzb img, const Mask mask,
                                        short2* kpLoc, const unsigned int maxKeypoints,
                                        PtrStepi score, const int threshold){
    ...
    const int j = threadIdx.x + blockIdx.x * blockDim.x + 3;
    const int i = threadIdx.y + blockIdx.y * blockDim.y + 3;

    if (i < img.rows - 3 && j < img.cols - 3 && mask(i, j))
    {
        int v;
        uint C[4] = {0,0,0,0};
        C[2] |= static_cast<uint>(img(i - 3, j - 1)) << 8;
        C[2] |= static_cast<uint>(img(i - 3, j));
        ...
        int d1 = diffType(v, C[1] & 0xff, threshold);
        int d2 = diffType(v, C[3] & 0xff, threshold);
        ...
        C[0] |= static_cast<uint>(img(i + 3, j + 1)) << 8;

        int mask1 = 0;
        int mask2 = 0;

        calcMask(C, v, threshold, mask1, mask2);

        if (isKeyPoint(mask1, mask2))
        {
            ...
        }
    }
}
```

---

[224] `__popc` - NVIDIA - http://docs.nvidia.com/cuda/cuda-math-api/group__CUDA__MATH__INTRINSIC__INT.html#group__CUDA__MATH__INTRINSIC__INT_1g01a673dffc6cbdbd73759d498b67e684

[225] Hamming Weight - Wikipedia - https://en.wikipedia.org/wiki/Hamming_weight

[226] How to count the number of set bits in a 32-bit integer? - StackOverflow - http://stackoverflow.com/a/109025/3671330

[227] OpenCV FAST features CUDA source code - `calcKeypoints` - https://github.com/Itseez/opencv/blob/3.0.0/modules/cudafeatures2d/src/cuda/fast.cu#L221

```
        ...
}
```

> It checks that the kernel is run inside a certain border, having a width of 3 pixels. In RenderScript, this behaviour can be defined on the Java side, using a `Script.LaunchOptions` object. This way, less kernel functions will be run and no boundary check will be needed:

```
Script.LaunchOptions fastLaunchOptions = new Script.LaunchOptions();
fastLaunchOptions.setX(3, inputImageSize.width - 3);
fastLaunchOptions.setY(3, inputImageSize.height - 3);
...
// E.g. usage
scriptCFastOpenCV.forEach_fastOpenCV(grayAllocation, fastKpAllocation, fastLaunchOptions);
```

> It defines the C[] array, which can be easily packed in an `int4` struct, remembering that elements are packed in `0=x,1=y,2=z,3=w` order:

```
uint4 C = {0,0,0,0};
C.z |= (uint)(rsGetElementAt_uchar(grayAllocation, x - 1, y - 3)) << 8;
C.z |= (uint)(rsGetElementAt_uchar(grayAllocation, x, y - 3));
...
int d1 = diffType(v, C.y & 0xff, fastThreshold);
```

> It uses the `static_cast<uint>()` function to retrieve pixel values. On the RenderScript side, this can be translated using the `rsGetElementAt_uchar` function:

```
C.z |= (uint)(rsGetElementAt_uchar(grayAllocation, x - 1, y - 3)) << 8;
C.z |= (uint)(rsGetElementAt_uchar(grayAllocation, x, y - 3));
...
v = (int) (rsGetElementAt_uchar(grayAllocation, x, y));
```

> `mask1` and `mask2` have to be packed, as seen before, into an `int2` struct, to enable the usage of the `calcMask` function, which relies on pointers:

```
int2 mask = calcMask(C, v, fastThreshold);

if (isKeyPoint(mask)) {
    return 1;
}

return 0;
```

> As said before, scoring functions invocation will be skipped.

The final conversion result is as follows:

```
uchar __attribute__((kernel)) fastOpenCV(uchar in, uint x, uint y){
    int v;
    uint4 C = {0,0,0,0};

    C.z |= (uint)(rsGetElementAt_uchar(grayAllocation, x - 1, y - 3)) << 8;
    ...
    v = (int) (rsGetElementAt_uchar(grayAllocation, x, y));
    C.y |= (uint)(rsGetElementAt_uchar(grayAllocation, x + 3, y));

    int d1 = diffType(v, C.y & 0xff, fastThreshold);
    int d2 = diffType(v, C.w & 0xff, fastThreshold);

    if ((d1 | d2) == 0){
        return 0;
    }
```

```
C.w |= (uint)(rsGetElementAt_uchar(grayAllocation, x - 3, y + 1)) << 8;
...
C.x |= (uint)(rsGetElementAt_uchar(grayAllocation, x + 1, y + 3)) << 8;

int2 mask = calcMask(C, v, fastThreshold);

if (isKeyPoint(mask)) {
    return 1;
}

return 0;
}
```

The kernel can now be invoked on the Java side. The required elements are the same as for the original FAST library:

> grayAllocation, the allocation containing the input grayscale image.
> fastKpAllocation, the allocation that will contain the algorithm results.

Invocation can be done with the following code:

```
scriptCFastOpenCV.forEach_fastOpenCV(grayAllocation, fastKpAllocation, fastLaunchOptions);
```

Porting - conclusions

C libraries (and, to some degree, even C++ ones) can be translated to work inside RenderScript without too much effort, because they share the same language mechanics. To be noticed is that portings are not always efficient: for example, some CUDA kernels are made to take full advantage of GPU's memory speed, which is higher than CPU's. On Android, this behavior can not be applied, because mobile devices have a shared memory architecture.

The comparison

The comparison objective is to demonstrate how faster RenderScript can operate when compared to non-GPU powered libraries. To achieve the purpose, the original FAST library implementation (its source code can be found in its homepage[228]), its RenderScript porting and OpenCV RenderScript porting are going to be used, running their 9 contiguous points version aside. Execution will then happen both on the CPU and on GPU sides and a comparison of running times will be logged.

Both implementations are evaluated with the same input and execute the same calculations. The input of both implementations is pre-processed using RenderScript (the camera images are converted to grayscale).

Input

Input data is a sequence of YUV images, captured in real-time, having a 1280x720 resolution.

CPU version

The CPU version is implemented inside the Android NDK (using the *external build process*), with the aid of OpenMP[229] library, which lets developers run function blocks in parallel (on all the CPU cores) with just a small code overhead.

GPU version

The GPU version offers two implementations:

> The direct porting of the *original C FAST library*.
> The porting of *OpenCV's CUDA FAST detection* implementation.

Results

By running the app (you're encouraged to test it on your devices), a common result is as follows (using a Samsung Galaxy Note 3[230]):

Task name	Task main operation	Is using RenderScript	Elapsed time (ms)
YUV to grayscale (RenderScriptIntrinsic)	Computation	Yes	13.348
YUV to grayscale (RenderScript)	Computation	Yes	**7.378**
YUV to grayscale (NDK)	Computation	No	48.190
RenderScript FAST lib	Memory access	Yes	**11.736**
RenderScript FAST (OpenCV porting)	Memory access	Yes	14.740
NDK FAST lib (optimized)	Memory access	No	16.058

It can be seen that RenderScript implementations perform faster than pure NDK ones in both memory access (FAST detection) and pure calculation (YUV to grayscale) tasks.

Even if timings are similar (in the range of some milliseconds, when talking about memory access), stressing the GPU instead of the CPU can provide huge benefits to every application, because in this way it is easier not to overkill the user interface with visual stuttering.

Further works - Scoring

Usually one needs to select the best points extracted from an image (for example, to limit the maximum number of detected points). This operation can be done when the points have a **score**, a value that explains how "good" a point is. To calculate this score there are various methods and, for FAST features, two are commonly used:

---

[228] FAST features - Edward Rosten - http://www.edwardrosten.com/work/fast.htm
[229] OpenMP - http://openmp.org/
[230] Samsung Galaxy Note 3 - GSMArena - http://www.gsmarena.com/samsung_galaxy_note_3-5665.php

> The Harris corner detector[231] is a good and strong scoring method. A sample code for this calculation can be found inside the OpenCV ORB extractor code[232].

> The FAST scoring[233] method is lightweight and based on the FAST threshold.

The porting of these methods can follow the same aforementioned process as the FAST features detector.

Conclusions

This chapter provided an example of how the porting process of a C/C++ library on RenderScript can be done. It is not always a straightforward task, mostly because it can be necessary to rewrite/implement different routines. The results, however, are encouraging: when dealing with large sets of data, like images, RenderScript works just perfectly.

---

[231] Harris corner detector - OpenCV -
http://docs.opencv.org/2.4/doc/tutorials/features2d/trackingmotion/harris_detector/harris_detector.html
[232] OpenCV ORB extractor code - https://github.com/Itseez/opencv/blob/3.0.0/modules/features2d/src/orb.cpp#L130
[233] FAST scoring - OpenCV - https://github.com/Itseez/opencv/blob/3.0.0/modules/cudafeatures2d/src/cuda/fast.cu#L195

Conclusions

RenderScript proves itself to be a useful and easy-to-work-with parallel computing framework.

The following are some thoughts about RenderScript, referring to the latest available current version (API 23).

The framework

Pros: what is good about RenderScript?

> Being based upon a C99-like language, RenderScript provides a common way of writing functions and logic.
> Setting up RenderScript elements on the Java side is straightforward.
> Performance can be extremely good when device-specific drivers are provided.
> Performance is still good when device-specific drivers are not provided, compared to bare NDK usage.

Cons: what can be improved?

> The NDK C++ side support is still limited, not supporting custom `struct` elements.
> Functions to get contents of variables and custom `struct` elements are not available, despite being available inside the `libRS.so` library.
> It is not possible to directly implement C++-like code, containing classes, interfaces and other Object Oriented Programming[234] paradigms. This missing feature can cause some problems when dealing with porting operations from other parallel computing frameworks like CUDA.

The book

This book explained:

> RenderScript basics, like what elements it provides to developers and how to put them to work together.
> A discussion over performance, dealing both with devices (high or low end ones) and techniques (e.g. using pointers or FilterScript).
> An overview of what lies underneath RenderScript's Java side: what happens when RenderScript functions are called, how the NDK side works and how to directly invoke RenderScript's library methods.
> Different examples to show how RenderScript can be applied to different scenarios. The knowledge covered by such examples gives developers different points of view of this beautiful framework, and should inspire them to apply RenderScript to many other topics.
> A special example, the FAST features detector porting, to show how a conversion from CUDA to RenderScript can be done.

Possible further applications of RenderScript, which are intended for a mobile-related world, reside in:

> Sound analysis (Digital Signal Processing[235]).
> Wearable devices raw signals analysis, like Electromyography[236] data (e.g. provided by MYO[237] armband), Electroencephalography[238] data (e.g. provided by Emotiv EPOC / EPOC+[239]).
> Advanced image processing, like Multi Face Detection and Recognition[240].
> Neural networks[241] testing on mobile-phones, which would require a large number of parallel processes.

---

[234] Object Oriented Programming - Wikibooks - https://en.wikibooks.org/wiki/Object_Oriented_Programming
[235] Digital Signal Processing - Wikipedia - https://en.wikipedia.org/wiki/Digital_signal_processing
[236] Electromyography - Wikipedia - https://en.wikipedia.org/wiki/Electromyography
[237] MYO - https://www.myo.com/
[238] Electroencephalography - Wikipedia - https://en.wikipedia.org/wiki/Electroencephalography
[239] Emotiv EPOC / EPOC+ - https://emotiv.com/epoc.php
[240] Varun Pande, Khaled Elleithy, Laiali Almazaydeh - Parallel Processing for Multi Face Detection and Recognition - https://www.researchgate.net/publication/256455704_Parallel_Processing_for_Multi_Face_Detection_and_Recognition

What is missing?

This book covered many arguments, but not all of them. A list of missing topics can be as follows:

> The `ScriptGroup`[242] class has not been described because the recent transition to Android 23, which deprecated the `ScriptGroup.Builder` class in favor of the `ScriptGroup.Builder2` one, has not yet been thoroughly analyzed. Its possible impact on performance could be a topic of discussion in the *Performance notes* chapter, *Kernels calling* section.

> The `Allocation.OnBufferAvailableListener`[243] interface, which can be used to connect the camera2[244] package to RenderScript, has not been tested yet. It is possible to find an example of its usage inside Android source code[245].

The above topics could be covered in a future edition of this book.

---

[241] MIT - Energy-friendly chip can perform powerful artificial-intelligence tasks - http://news.mit.edu/2016/neural-chip-artificial-intelligence-mobile-devices-0203

[242] Android Developers - `ScriptGroup` - http://developer.android.com/reference/android/renderscript/ScriptGroup.html

[243] Android Developers - `Allocation.OnBufferAvailableListener` - http://developer.android.com/reference/android/renderscript/Allocation.OnBufferAvailableListener.html

[244] Android Developers - `camera2` - http://developer.android.com/reference/android/hardware/camera2/package-summary.html

[245] Android source code - `camera2` test - https://android.googlesource.com/platform/cts/+/marshmallow-mr1-release/tests/tests/hardware/src/android/hardware/camera2/cts/rs/BlockingInputAllocation.java

Appendix - API changes

With Android API evolving year-to-year, additional functions have been added to the RenderScript system. In this book I focused on API 18 because it was the lowest API version that guaranteed the best support to common functions.

Exploring Android API differences tables[246], it's possible to understand what every new Android version brought in (look for package android.renderscript).

When, in the following list, it is said that RenderScript script-functions get added, it is necessary to build your project using at least the renderscriptTargetApi value corresponding to the current evaluated API level.

Below are some lists of relevant changes (author's judgment comes in here!):

API 19[247]

> Support for ScriptIntrinsicHistogram[248] added. This intrinsic built class lets you calculate a histogram of a uchar or uchar4 Allocation. Calculating a histogram[249] is useful when, for example, you need to understand whether an image is over-exposed or under-exposed[250].
> Allocation.OnBufferAvailableListener[251] class added. This is useful when you are using an Allocation with the USAGE_IO_INPUT flag, and your input source makes data available. As can be seen from Android source code[252], OnBufferAvailableListener can be used with camera2 package, which was introduced in API 21.
> ScriptIntrinsicColorMatrix[253] class added.
> clamp script-functions have been added, now accepting parameters other than float.

API 20[254]

> ScriptIntrinsicResize[255] class added. This class can help you resize an image bicubically.
> rsAtomic script-functions have been extended to atomically change even uint32_t variables. Earlier they could change only int32_t ones.

API 21[256]

> The following methods have been added to the Allocation class:

```
void copy1DRangeFrom(int, int, Object)
void copy1DRangeFromUnchecked(int, int, Object)
void copy2DRangeFrom(int, int, int, int, Object)
void copyFrom(Object)
void copyFromUnchecked(Object)
void copyTo(Object)
```

---

[246] Android Developers - Android API differences tables - https://developer.android.com/sdk/api_diff/19/changes.html
[247] API 19 - https://developer.android.com/sdk/api_diff/19/changes.html
[248] Android Developers - ScriptIntrinsicHistogram - https://developer.android.com/reference/android/renderscript/ScriptIntrinsicHistogram.html
[249] Image histogram - Wikipedia - https://en.wikipedia.org/wiki/Image_histogram
[250] How to Read and Use Histograms - http://digital-photography-school.com/how-to-read-and-use-histograms/
[251] Android Developers - Allocation.OnBufferAvailableListener - https://developer.android.com/reference/android/renderscript/Allocation.OnBufferAvailableListener.html
[252] Android source code - camera2 test - https://android.googlesource.com/platform/cts/+/marshmallow-release/tests/tests/hardware/src/android/hardware/camera2/cts/rs/BlockingInputAllocation.java
[253] Android Developers - ScriptIntrinsicColorMatrix - https://developer.android.com/sdk/api_diff/19/changes/android.renderscript.ScriptIntrinsicColorMatrix.html
[254] API 20 - https://developer.android.com/sdk/api_diff/20/changes.html
[255] Android Developers - ScriptIntrinsicResize - https://developer.android.com/reference/android/renderscript/ScriptIntrinsicResize.html
[256] API 21 - https://developer.android.com/sdk/api_diff/21/changes.html

> Flags like `CREATE_FLAG_LOW_LATENCY` have been added. Their implementation varies from device to device, and it is not possible to be certain that they work flawlessly.
> Utility functions have been added to the Type class, to instantiate types faster than using `Type.Builder`:

```
Type createX(RenderScript, Element, int)
Type createXY(RenderScript, Element, int, int)
Type createXYZ(RenderScript, Element, int, int, int)
```

> The support for custom user data in the `rsforEach` function has been dropped, as seen in `api/rs_for_each.spec`[257], where the max renderscriptTargetApi version to use it is 20. From 21 onwards, for now (with Android Marshmallow), the only available `rsForEach` call is:

```
#if (defined(RS_VERSION) && (RS_VERSION >= 14))
extern void __attribute__((overloadable))
    rsForEach(rs_script script, rs_allocation input, rs_allocation output);
#endif
```

> `convert_` script-functions have been added, to convert `long` and `double` elements. E.g.: `convert_double3`.
> Many `native_` script-functions have been added, accepting vectors as arguments. Full math reference can be seen in the `api/rs_math.spec`[258] file.

API 22[259]

> `rsAllocationVLoadX` and `rsAllocationVStoreX` script-functions got introduced, to retrieve and store a vector from and to an allocation made of scalar values:

```
// myAllocation contains: 1, 2, 3, 4, 5, 6, 7

// Will return a int3 from an allocation made only of integers (not packed).
// Will contain idx, idx+1 and idx+2 elements.
int3 myVector = rsAllocationVLoadX_int3(myAllocation, 0);

// myVector contains: 1, 2, 3

// Set the vector back into the allocation, into another starting index
rsAllocationVStoreX_int3(myAllocation, myVector, 4);

// Now, myAllocation contains: 1, 2, 3, 4, 1, 2, 3
```

> Unsafe `rsGetAllocation(const void* p)` script-function got deprecated.

API 23[260]

> The `ScriptIntrinsicBLAS`[261] class was added. It can be used to perform tons of mathematical calculations of different kinds, belonging to the Basic Linear Algebra Subprograms[262] functions set.
> Copy range to functions have been added to the `Allocation` class:

```
void copy1DRangeTo(int, int, byte[])
void copy1DRangeTo(int, int, float[])
```

---

[257] RenderScript source code - `api/rs_for_each.spec` -
https://android.googlesource.com/platform/frameworks/rs/+/marshmallow-mr1-release/api/rs_for_each.spec#142
[258] RenderScript source code - `api/rs_math.spec` - https://android.googlesource.com/platform/frameworks/rs/+/marshmallow-mr1-release/api/rs_math.spec
[259] API 22 - https://developer.android.com/sdk/api_diff/22/changes.html
[260] API 23 - https://developer.android.com/sdk/api_diff/23/changes.html
[261] Android Developers - `ScriptIntrinsicBLAS` -
https://developer.android.com/reference/android/renderscript/ScriptIntrinsicBLAS.html
[262] Basic Linear Algebra Subprograms - http://www.netlib.org/blas/

```
void copy1DRangeTo(int, int, int[])
void copy1DRangeTo(int, int, Object)
void copy1DRangeTo(int, int, short[])
void copy1DRangeToUnchecked(int, int, byte[])
void copy1DRangeToUnchecked(int, int, float[])
void copy1DRangeToUnchecked(int, int, int[])
void copy1DRangeToUnchecked(int, int, Object)
void copy1DRangeToUnchecked(int, int, short[])
void copy2DRangeTo(int, int, int, int, byte[])
void copy2DRangeTo(int, int, int, int, float[])
void copy2DRangeTo(int, int, int, int, int[])
void copy2DRangeTo(int, int, int, int, Object)
void copy2DRangeTo(int, int, int, int, short[])
void copy3DRangeTo(int, int, int, int, int, int, Object)
```

> Copy 3D range `from` functions have been added to the `Allocation` class:

```
void copy3DRangeFrom(int, int, int, int, int, int, Allocation, int, int, int)
void copy3DRangeFrom(int, int, int, int, int, int, Object)
```

> Half element (floating point, 16 bit) has been created: `Element F16(RenderScript)`.
> `rs_kernel_context` script-type has been added. It can be used, together with script-functions like `rsGetDimX`, to retrieve relevant information about current kernel execution. For example, citing directly RenderScript's `api/rs_for_each.spec`[263]:

```
/*
 * rsGetDimX: Size of the X dimension for the specified context
 *
 * Returns the size of the X dimension for the specified context.
 *
 * This context is created when a kernel is launched. It contains common
 * characteristics of the allocations being iterated over by the kernel
 * in a very efficient structure.  It also contains rarely used indexes.
 *
 * You can access it by adding a special parameter named "context" and of
 * type rs_kernel_context to your kernel function.  E.g.
 * int4 RS_KERNEL myKernel(int4 value, rs_kernel_context context) {
 *    uint32_t size = rsGetDimX(context); //...
 *
 * To get the dimension of specific allocation,
 * use rsAllocationGetDimX().
 */
#if (defined(RS_VERSION) && (RS_VERSION >= 23))
extern uint32_t __attribute__((overloadable))
    rsGetDimX(rs_kernel_context context);
#endif
```

> The RenderScript graphics subsystem got deprecated. It won't work at all on 64-bit devices, as stated in RenderScript's `api/rs_graphics.spec`[264].

---

[263] RenderScript source code - `api/rs_for_each.spec` -
https://android.googlesource.com/platform/frameworks/rs/+/marshmallow-mr1-release/api/rs_for_each.spec#313
[264] RenderScript source code - `api/rs_graphics.spec` -
https://android.googlesource.com/platform/frameworks/rs/+/marshmallow-mr1-release/api/rs_graphics.spec#22

Appendix: Enable NDK support

To enable the NDK support for your project, there are at least two main ways, depending on what you need:

> Simple implementation, when you need to run code that does not depend on external libraries and too many custom compiling flags.
> External rock-solid `ndk-build` building, that lets you use `Android.mk`[265] and `Application.mk`[266] files.

Note: tons of samples regarding the Android NDK can be found inside Google samples' GitHub repository[267].

Install NDK

First of all, if you don't have the NDK installed, you need to install it:

1. Open the **Android SDK Manager**.

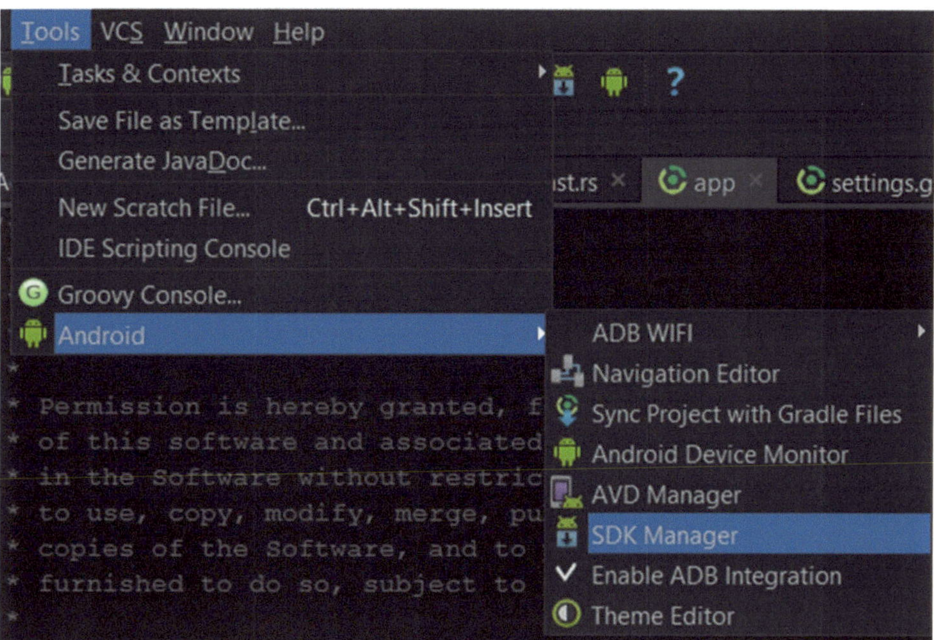

Open SDK Manager

2. Under **SDK Tools** tab, check **Android NDK**, click on **OK**, confirm that you want to install the component and wait for it to be downloaded.

---

[265] Android Developers - `Android.mk` - http://developer.android.com/ndk/guides/android_mk.html
[266] Android Developers - `Application.mk` - http://developer.android.com/ndk/guides/application_mk.html
[267] Google samples' GitHub repository - https://github.com/googlesamples/android-ndk

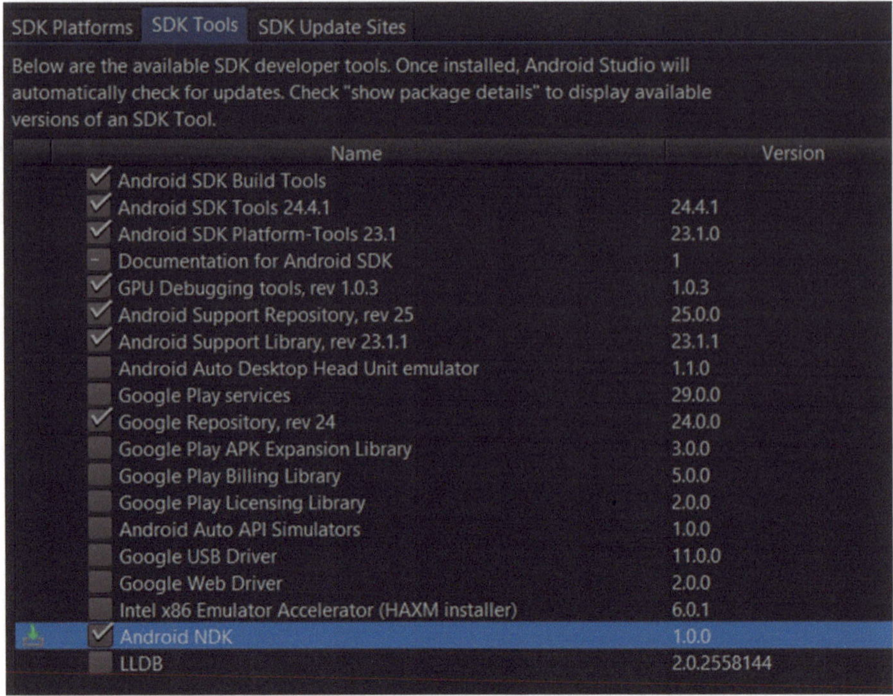

Android NDK

3. Now, the NDK will be automatically referred in projects that require it.

Note: for your info, the default NDK installation path is a folder named ndk-bundle or ndk, placed directly inside your Android SDK folder. You can find your SDK location by looking at the top of **SDK Manager** window:

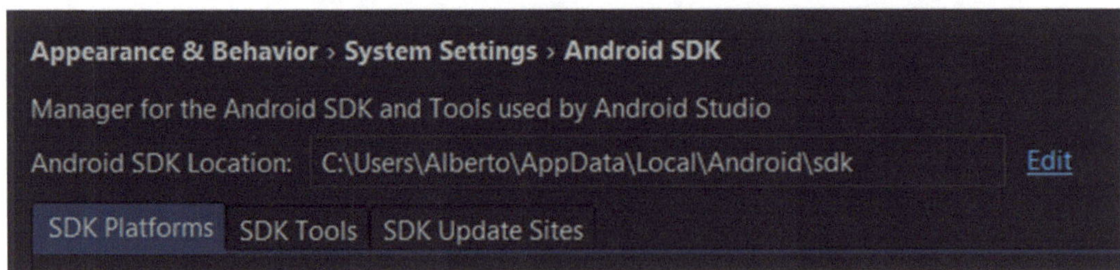

SDK location

Simple implementation

Be sure that you are using Gradle > 2.5 and Android Studio > 1.4:

1. Create a new Native Run configuration by:
    1. Open the **Edit Configurations** window.

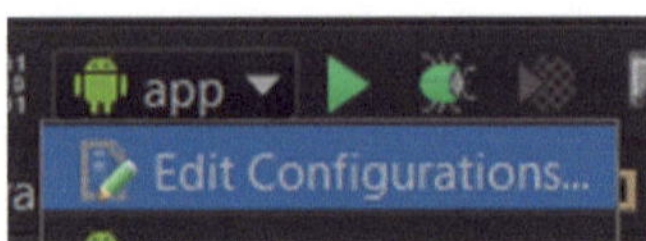

Edit Configurations

2. Add an **Android Native** configuration.

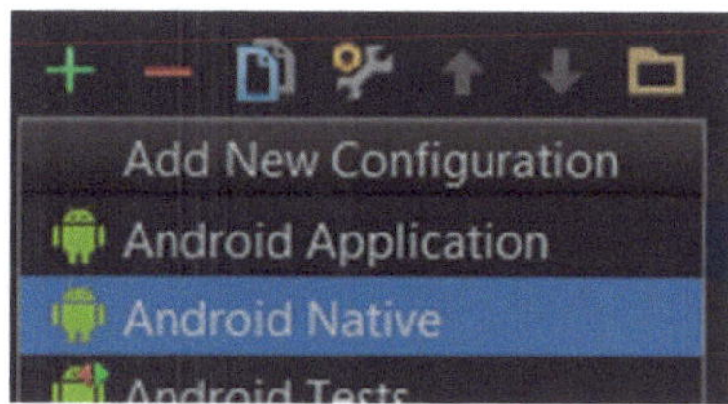

Native Activity

3. Select your app module.

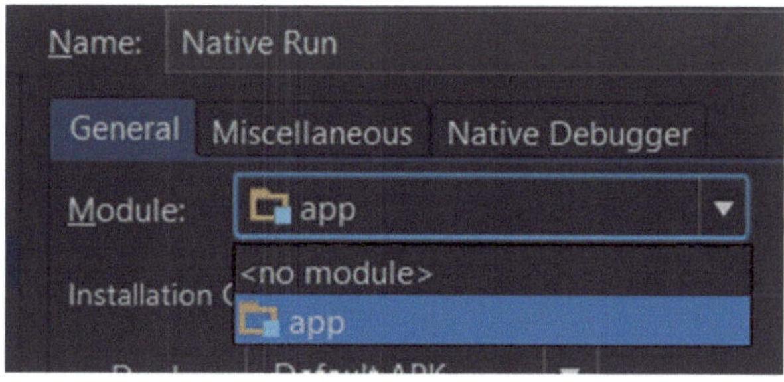

App module

4. Click on **Ok**.
5. If an error message appears, click on **Setup NDK**, otherwise go to step 2.

NDK Error

6. Click on **Ok** to download the latest Android NDK (or select a folder if you already have it. If you downloaded it with the **SDK Manager**, the ndk folder will probably be inside your Android SDK main folder).

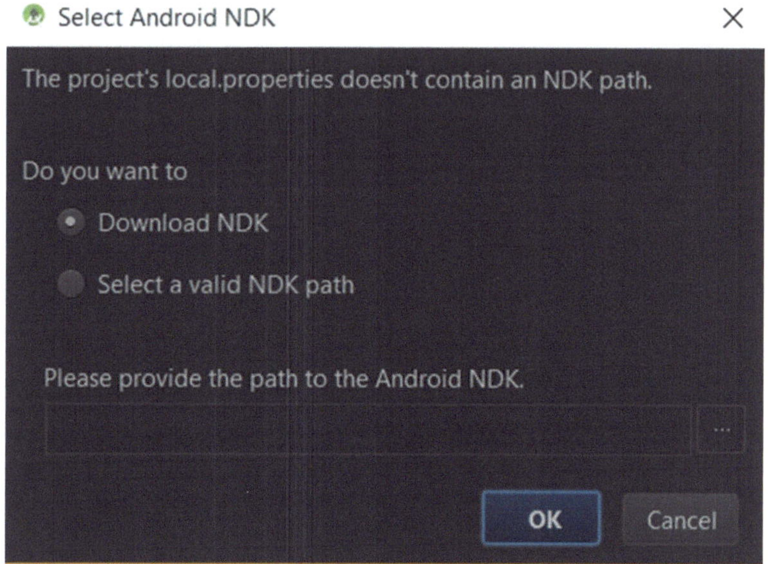

Download NDK

2. Edit your app `build.gradle` file, adding the following contents:
    1. Inside the `android.buildTypes.release` section:

```
ndk {
    debuggable = true
}
```

2. Inside the `android.buildTypes.debug` section (create it if not exists):

```
ndk {
    debuggable = true
    jniDebuggable = true
}
```

3. Inside the `android.defaultConfig` section:

```
ndk {
    moduleName = "native"
}
```

3. Edit your `gradle.properties` file and add the following line:

```
android.useDeprecatedNdk=true
```

4. Create a new JNI folder.

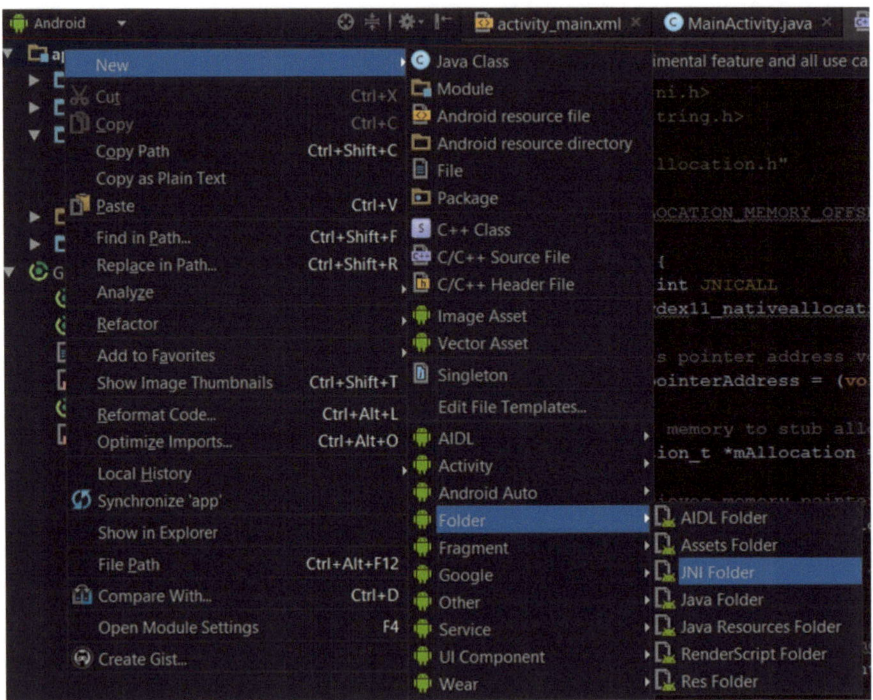

New JNI folder

5. Add a new C++ file.

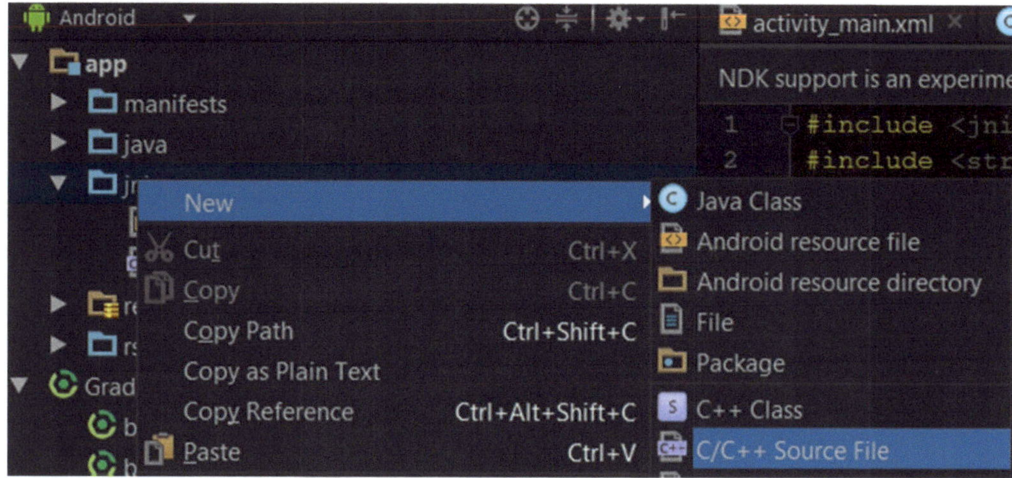

New cpp file

6. Here you have your project set up to use Android NDK.

External ndk-build implementation

The external ndk-build implementations makes the `ndk-build` script perform the NDK code compiling, instead of Android Studio. Benefits are achieved in terms of performance and customization.

You can find an example of this process inside the RSNDKExample sample project[268].

1. Open the `build.gradle` file relative to your module.
2. Add the following line to its header:

```
// Used to detect if we are using Windows or Linux
// or whatever else
import org.apache.tools.ant.taskdefs.condition.Os;
```

3. Append, to the end of android section:

```
// This settings tells Android Studio where to look for NDK
// built libraries
sourceSets.main {
    // Sets location where Android Studio will look for
    // .so library files (output of ndk-build)
    jniLibs.srcDir 'src/main/libs'
}

// Calls regular ndk-build(.cmd) script from app directory
task ndkBuild(type: Exec) {
    // If you are creating a library, and you have defined
    // apply plugin: 'com.android.library', please change the following
    // key 'com.android.application' to 'com.android.library'
    def ndkDir = project.plugins.findPlugin('com.android.application').sdkHandler.getNdkFolder()

    def ndkBuild = ""
    if(Os.isFamily(Os.FAMILY_WINDOWS))
    {
        ndkBuild = "$ndkDir\\ndk-build.cmd"
    }
    else
```

---

268 RSNDKExample sample project - https://bitbucket.org/cmaster11/rsbookexamples/src/tip/RSNDKExample/

```
{
    ndkBuild = "$ndkDir/ndk-build"
}

commandLine "$ndkBuild", "NDK_PROJECT_PATH=build/intermediates/ndk",
        // Output libraries folder
        "NDK_LIBS_OUT=src/main/libs",
        // Android.mk file location (omit if not needed)
        "APP_BUILD_SCRIPT=src/main/jni/Android.mk",
        // Application.mk file location (omit if not needed)
        "NDK_APPLICATION_MK=src/main/jni/Application.mk",
        // Verbose, just to better understand what happens
        "V=1"

}


// NDK build task must execute before Java compile one
tasks.withType(JavaCompile) {
    compileTask -> compileTask.dependsOn ndkBuild
}
```

4. Append, at the end of the file, the following code:

```
// Disables Android Studio automatic compile of NDK code
afterEvaluate {
    tasks.getByName("compileReleaseNdk").each { task ->
        task.enabled = false
    }
    tasks.getByName("compileDebugNdk").each { task ->
        task.enabled = false
    }
}
```

5. Create a new JNI folder.

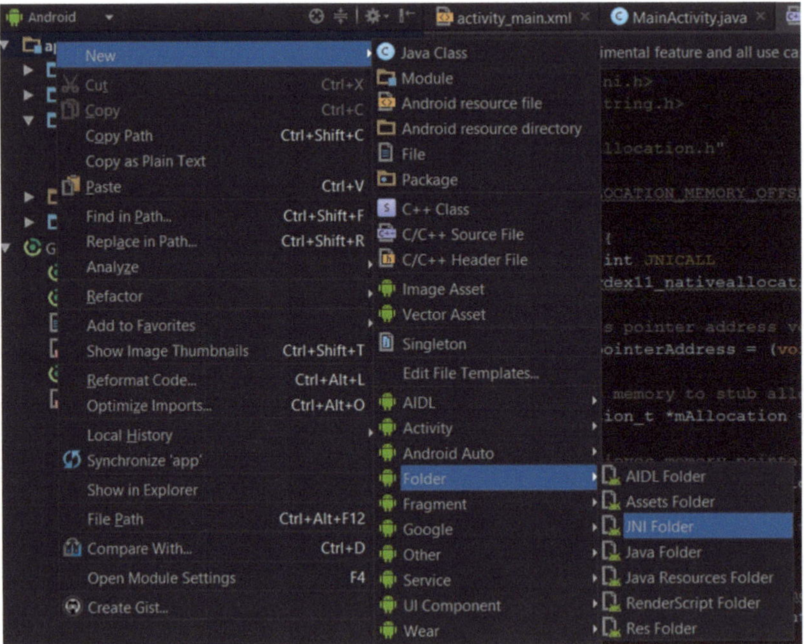

New JNI folder

6. Place your NDK code in the `src/main/jni` directory.

7. When building your project, the NDK side will be built automatically by Gradle.

Note: if the following error appears

```
A problem occurred starting process 'command 'null/ndk-build'
```

you have to manually set your NDK path inside `local.properties` file. Ex:

> Linux: `ndk.dir=/opt/android/ndk/android-ndk-r10e`
> Windows: `ndk.dir=D\:\\android-ndk-r10e`

Appendix: Other Android parallel computing frameworks

At the time of researching this topic (March, 2016), at least the following frameworks/systems can be found, that can let developers perform parallel computing operations on Android:

OpenGL ES[269]

OpenGL ES is the current de-facto standard framework for mobile devices graphics. It is able to run kernels, written in GLSL language[270], to perform calculations on the pure GPU side. Starting from version 3.1[271], compute shaders have been made available.

It offers benefits, when talking about both performance and cross-compatibility, because built kernels can be shared among different OSs (like Android, iOS, etc..). Also, it can be used directly inside the Java environment, without the need to use the Android NDK. One big drawback is its learning curve, which is steep for those who have never touched similar concepts.

A drawback on Android is that, as stated in the OpenGL ES Android homepage[272], support for version 3.1 starts with Android 21 (Lollipop).

Links:

> ARM - Get started with compute shaders[273].
> Mali Developer Center - Introduction to compute shaders[274].

OpenCL[275]

OpenCL is a cross-platform parallel computing framework. Its implementation on Android is device-specific (dependent upon the device manufacturer), and it is not directly accessible from the Java side (NDK usage is required). It is necessary to create device-specific builds[276] and not all devices support this. To see a list of devices that support OpenCL, please refer to the OpenCL-Z homepage[277] (OpenCL-Z is an Android app that checks whether or not a certain device supports OpenCL, and results are logged in the website) or the ArrayFire library OpenCL section[278].

A drawback of this framework is that Google is publicly stating[279] its desire to support the evolution of RenderScript instead of the OpenCL one.

Links:

> Intel - Getting Started with OpenCL™ on Android OS[280].

---

[269] OpenGL ES - https://www.khronos.org/opengles/
[270] GLSL language - Wikipedia - https://en.wikipedia.org/wiki/OpenGL_Shading_Language
[271] Khronos Releases OpenGL ES 3.1 Specification - https://www.khronos.org/news/press/khronos-releases-opengl-es-3.1-specification
[272] OpenGL ES Android homepage - http://developer.android.com/guide/topics/graphics/opengl.html
[273] ARM - Get started with compute shaders - https://community.arm.com/groups/arm-mali-graphics/blog/2014/04/17/get-started-with-compute-shaders
[274] Mali Developer Center - Introduction to compute shaders - http://malideveloper.arm.com/downloads/deved/tutorial/SDK/linux/2.4.4/html/compute_intro.html
[275] OpenCL - https://www.khronos.org/opencl/
[276] Using OpenCL in the new Android Studio - StackOverflow - http://stackoverflow.com/a/32153252/3671330
[277] OpenCL-Z homepage - http://web.guohuiwang.com/software/opencl_z_android
[278] ArrayFire library OpenCL section - http://arrayfire.com/opencl-on-mobile-devices/
[279] Why did Google choose RenderScript instead of OpenCL - StackOverflow - http://stackoverflow.com/questions/14385843/why-did-google-choose-renderscript-instead-of-opencl/14389506#14389506
[280] Intel - Getting Started with OpenCL™ on Android OS - https://software.intel.com/en-us/android/articles/opencl-basic-sample-for-android-os

Vulkan[281]

Vulkan is a newborn (released on February 16th, 2016), cross-platform framework, built to perform graphics and parallel computing operations. Its minimum target is Android 23 (Marshmallow), and it requires device-specific support.

Vulkan got developed to overcome OpenGL architecture limitations, to focus on lower battery drain (at the same time improving the performance) and provide better developing experience.

Links:

> Khronos Vulkan Registry[282].
> NVIDIA - Getting Started with Vulkan on Android[283].

CUDA[284] (Only for Tegra-powered[285] devices)

CUDA is NVIDIA's parallel computing platform, which lets users write kernels in C/C++ language. It requires compatible hardware, like NVIDIA Tegra[286] chipsets.

Links:

> NVIDIA CUDA for Android[287]

---

[281] Vulkan - https://www.khronos.org/vulkan/
[282] Khronos Vulkan Registry - https://www.khronos.org/registry/vulkan/
[283] NVIDIA - Getting Started with Vulkan on Android - https://developer.nvidia.com/vulkan-android
[284] CUDA - http://www.nvidia.com/object/cuda_home_new.html
[285] Tegra-powered - https://developer.nvidia.com/codeworks-android#Devices
[286] NVIDIA Tegra - http://www.nvidia.com/object/tegra.html
[287] NVIDIA CUDA for Android - http://docs.nvidia.com/gameworks/index.html#technologies/mobile/cuda_android_main.htm

9 791220 011303